I0105996

Beginning Zen Buddhism

*Timeless Teachings to Master Your Emotions,
Reduce Stress and Anxiety, and Achieve Inner Peace*

Beginning Zen Buddhism

PUBLISHED BY: Amy White
©Copyright 2020 - All rights reserved.

All rights reserved. No part of this publication may be reproduced, distributed, or transmitted in any form or by any means, including photocopying, recording, or other electronic or mechanical methods, without the prior written permission of the publisher, except in the case of brief quotations embodied in critical reviews and certain other noncommercial uses permitted by copyright law.

Under no circumstances will any blame or legal responsibility be held against the publisher, or author, for any damages, reparation, or monetary loss due to the information contained within this book, either directly or indirectly.

Legal Notice:

This book is copyright protected. It is only for personal use. You cannot amend, distribute, sell, use, quote or paraphrase any part, or the content within this book, without the consent of the author or publisher.

Disclaimer Notice:

Please note the information contained within this document is for educational and entertainment purposes only. All effort has been executed to present accurate, up to date, reliable, complete information. No warranties of any kind are declared or implied. Readers acknowledge that the author is not engaged in the rendering of legal, financial, medical or professional advice. The content within this book has been derived from various sources. Please consult a licensed professional before attempting any techniques outlined in this book.

By reading this document, the reader agrees that under no circumstances is the author responsible for any losses, direct or indirect, that are incurred as a result of the use of the information contained within this document, including, but not limited to, errors, omissions, or inaccuracies.

Table Of Contents

Your Free Gift

As a way of saying thanks for your purchase, I want to offer you a free bonus e-Book called *7 Essential Mindfulness Habits* exclusive to the readers of this book.

To get instant access just go to:

https://theartofmastery.com/mindfulness

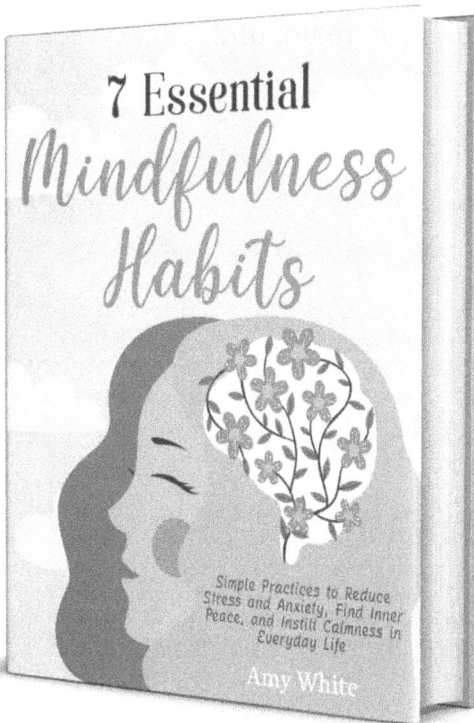

Inside the book, you will discover:

- What is mindfulness meditation
- Why mindfulness is so effective in reducing stress and increasing joy, composure, and serenity
- Various mindfulness techniques that you can do anytime, anywhere
- 7 essential mindfulness habits to implement starting today
- Tips and fun activities to teach your kids to be more mindful

Introduction

Why do some people move on faster than others? Why are most people having a hard time coping with life's stresses and problems? Why are we still unhappy despite all the success we have? These are some of the most common questions we often ask ourselves when faced with struggles and difficulties.

Coping with life might not be as easy as we imagine. We set goals and plans on how we should live our lives, but when reality hits back and goes a different direction, we become confused and anxious. Each of us has personal issues, secrets, dreams, and desires. In most cases, one of them will eat us up, and we tend to lose focus on how to balance our lives.

I remember a good friend whose story fits well here. Charlie lost his father at a very young age. He fondly remembers going to music festivals together where he and his dad would dance and sing to the rhythm of the songs. They shared a really close relationship, and life was never the same.

Charlie was a smart kid; his mom never had problems with his grades and behavior at school. But growing up with a single parent practically meant raising himself. Everything seemed fine until he became an adult, met new people, saw new places, and tried new hobbies.

Going through life with very little guidance to shape his foundations took its toll. Charlie spent most of his time in bars, concerts, and parties, both with friends and strangers, smoking, drinking, and taking drugs. He enjoyed his newfound freedom and the new things he was experiencing. Nothing mattered. It was fun and terrible at the same time, but it also led to a turning point in his life.

When he was 21, he joined a marathon and fractured his ankle during the race. Charlie was then brought to a hospital to have it checked. As he sat quietly but annoyed by the situation, he saw an old man lying in bed, talking to a young lady. The elderly man looked weak and appeared to be crying. Minutes later, the man died. Seeing that brought him back to the day when his father passed. It was like a switch flipped, and just like that, Charlie felt human again. It was weird, but he found it to be one of the most remarkable moments in his life.

Looking back, Charlie realized that life wasn't really that complicated. As many years as a person can be blessed to live, it will feel short and simple towards the end. We are born, we grow up, we live, and then we die. However, in his case, it was ironic to watch a person dying in the same place where fresh souls are being born.

There are quite a few factors in our life that affects our disposition. Every seemingly bad thing has a good counterpart, and our perception will ultimately play a key role in how we go through life.

End and change

Death is inevitable, and so is change—whether it be a change in relationships, status, appearance, and whatnot, it will happen. The secret to conquering these things and achieving happiness and satisfaction comes from within, and we will talk about this more in the succeeding chapters of this book.

Life's challenges

When we were young, we were all told that things would always work out in the end, that everything would be just fine. But as we grew older and saw the world as it truly is, we realized that it doesn't always end well. Life will always throw curveballs and turn what was once mundane into a seemingly unending journey of struggles. These challenges are quite constant; they keep us on our toes. A perfect and conflict-free life is boring. The real challenge here is how we handle the situation. If you don't find your footing, you'll spiral away and find yourself in a losing battle all the time. Things can easily get overwhelming, and the line between rational and irrational decisions becomes blurry.

Distractions

Most of the time, we create problems for ourselves. Not intentionally, of course, but we do. Distractions are all around us, and sometimes, we allow these interferences to take over instead of taking control over the situation.

Typically, there are four types of problems people experience: simple, complicated, complex, and perplexing. We tend to spend all our energy worrying and complicating things. We must learn that problems are unique on their own, and each has a unique way of resolving.

This book could be the answer to all your doubts, questions, and dreams. It was written to serve as a testimony to life's realities, how to survive amidst all trials, and how to achieve real happiness despite suffering. The purpose of this book is not to create false hopes and promises to the readers; rather, it is meant to educate and open minds about how you can positively and beneficially change your life without the risks.

In the succeeding chapters, you will learn about the fundamentals of Buddhism and how its beliefs on life uncomplicate most situations. Understanding the principles behind Zen Buddhism will allow you to be fully in tune with the discipline to fully harness the benefits, practices, and how you can apply this to your daily life.

CHAPTER ONE

The Origin and Evolution of Zen Buddhism

"Your purpose in life

Is to find your purpose

And give your whole heart and soul to it."

-The Buddha

In the early centuries, Zen Buddhism was first brought to China by an Indian monk named Bodhidharma. It was during the 6th century that Taoism and Mahayana Buddhism were united, and Zen Buddhism was born.

Commonly called Chan Buddhism in China, it spread in different parts of the world. It was later brought to countries including Korea in the 7th century, Japan in the 12th century, and the West, where it became well-known during the mid-20th century.

Zen Buddhism was coined after "Zazen" and "Buddha," two significant aspects that contributed to the birth of Zen Buddhism.

If you look it up, *zazen* means "seated meditation," hence, it has another definition referred to as a deep intuitive understanding of the natural existence of things, including human life.

Buddha: The Enlightened One

Thousands of years ago, it was believed that there was once a simple yet noble man named Siddhartha Gautama, son of a king of the Shakya tribe, who was living a very abundant life with his family until he became conscious of the inevitable things all related to human beings and of the human life—sickness, aging, and death.

With an earnest desire to search for the truth, he then left his family and the palace, lived in forests, and went to different places where he met various people. He devoted all his time performing deep meditations, reflecting on his life's experiences, and deprived himself of any type of indulgence and earthly pleasure to show reverence to asceticism.

After a specific encounter with a monk, he decided to dedicate his life in search of peace and to resolve all issues on the suffering and death of the human being.

Motivated and hungered for solutions, Siddhartha Gautama studied and practiced all forms of philosophies previously existing. He went to prestigious philosophical and religious schools, which India had plenty of at that time, but none fulfilled him.

It was with desperation and strong willpower to answer his questions that he unquestionably sat down in *dhyana* posture, commonly called *zazen*, and contemplated. He decided to never move from his place until he untangled the mystery behind life and death. According to Buddhist writings, the Buddha did not move in his place under a Ficus religiosa tree for forty-nine days.

After mulling over everything—having to undergo oblivion and conquer his illusions—he found the most ultimate form of inner peace. He found it in his heart, breaking off the barrier between chaos and silence. It was during this time that he was called the Buddha or the Awakened One.

After being enlightened, the Buddha went to the Deer Park in Sarnath, where the holy city of Benares is. There, he had his first sermon, where he shared the subject of the Four Noble Truths.

Because of the genuineness of the *Dharma*, his teachings, he was able to capture the hearts of the people and convince them. He gathered five men who became his disciples later on. This marked the foundation of the Buddhist community.

The Buddha continued his meditations, illuminated his doubts, identified how suffering affected humans, and came up with a method on how one can free himself from it. At this point, he established the foundations of the philosophies that would be taught to generations throughout the years.

After the Buddha has passed away, his teachings began to spread and became the basis of today's Buddhism. More prominently in India, where it became the state religion, the followers of Buddhism established monasteries and advocated missionary works to areas in need.

As centuries passed, Buddhism eventually developed in other countries beyond India. Its philosophies and teachings were passed down in different interpretations contingent to the nation's diversity.

Today, the teachings of Zen Buddhism have reached many different parts of the world and greatly influenced many communities and believers. Three types of Buddhism were formed: Theravada Buddhism, Mahayana Buddhism, and Tibetan Buddhism, to represent particular geographical locations. Each type has its own interpretation and analysis of the Buddhist teachings. Thus, several topics have been linked to it, one of which is Zen Buddhism.

Many have lived by Zen Buddhism up to now, and countless people are still in pursuit of understanding it. With regards to this, we are all invited to start our journey towards a life of Zen by opening our minds and ourselves through the help of this book. In reading the full context, we are guided by the foundations of Zen Buddhism, how it affects our everyday life, and how we can walk the path towards enlightenment.

The followers of Buddhism do not recognize a god or a deity; instead, they virtuously focus on attaining enlightenment. Buddhism's founder and the Enlightened One is not a god. He is neither a son of a god nor a messenger from a god. The Buddha is a normal human being who exerted big efforts to acquire a deep interpretation and understanding of life. As a result, he was able to reach the highest form of state one can attain.

In this chapter, we have tackled the key points of Zen Buddhism, which are:

- Zen and Buddha are two important foundations of Zen Buddhism
- Zen Buddhism originated in China
- The term *Zen* was coined from the word *zazen*, meaning meditation
- Siddhartha Gautama is the Buddha, the Enlightened One
- Buddha is not a god; he is a real person
- The Buddha formed the concept of the Dharma, which will be discussed in the next chapters

CHAPTER TWO

Buddhism: Karma, Suffering, Nirvana, and Reincarnation

"As she has planted,

So does she harvest;

Such is the field of karma."

-Sri Guru Granth Sahib

The principle of Zen Buddhism tells that all human beings are Buddhas and that each one must be enlightened to discover the truth within him.

In a simpler context, to be a human being means to be a Buddha. The mere existence of a human person is already an indication of being a Buddha. The term *Buddha nature* is a definition of *human nature.*

You and I are Buddhas, and each one of us is capable of being enlightened.

During my early years in writing, I realized there is nothing more comforting than enlightening people's minds. Sharing thoughts while earning is incredible but being able to educate is another thing. It is a fulfillment that completes my well-being as an author.

The key concern of Zen is to perceive things as they are, plain and simple. It centers on things as to how they are in a natural state rather than on how and what we see it is. The term *Zen,* as I have stated previously, could have several meanings. It could be a school, a meditating position, or a calm state of mind. However, Zen Buddhism's central efforts are all about the significance of life.

By any means, Zen technically stands as an action; it is something one must do. It could not be explained through words; however, it must be experienced to be fully understood. In other standpoints, Zen is neither recognized as a philosophy nor a religion. It is considered as a meditation practice or an art of discovering self-freedom. To control the mind through meditation is the first step towards enlightening the inner self. Thus, other similar techniques are helpful to escape the mind from logical thinking and allow the mind to wander.

Understanding Karma

Have you done something bad to someone, then afterward, something bad also happened to you? You feel like you are paying for your unjust actions regardless of when or where you did it. It just comes right after you did something. Same as when you did something good, for some reason, you begin to receive help, or some luck comes along.

The law of Karma is a concept that states the relation of one's actions, speech, and thinking towards the aspect of one's life. It is a theory mostly recognized differently in Eastern religions.

Karma came from a Sanskrit word, which means "action." From the word itself, the concept of karma considerably follows the law of cause and effect for every action that has been done. Thus, if one lives or acts in a way that is against the natural harmony of things, for example, involving greed or anger, one may experience conflict or pain. This works the same thing on the other hand. When one's actions are inspired by love and kindness, the person then could possibly be repaid with kindness, such as getting help from other people in the future.

- Two Levels of Karma

There are two levels of how Karma can be understood. The first level, as explained above, is based on a cause and effect situation. When one performs an action, it is expected that he will begin to experience its consequences later on.

One approach of Buddhism in describing karma is its usage of metaphorical examples to describe how planting bad or good deeds could result in bad or good fruits. If you planted a good seed and took care of it very well, you will reap a good fruit in time.

In the second level, karma is based on how one perceives things. It primarily focuses on the quality of one's thoughts or state of mind. Understanding karma on this level comes naturally. When one acts or thinks with a happy state of mind, the person then feels a blissful atmosphere around him; therefore, happiness becoming the fruit of his thoughts.

From a Buddhist point of view, we are capable of facing karma even beyond our present life. This implies that bad actions made during the past or present life can cause bad results in the next life.

Karma serves an important role in a person's life after death. It determines what kind of life or status one will have in his next existence. Good karma can be portrayed as being reborn in a heavenly state or living an abundant life, while bad karma can cause a person to be disabled or miserable in his next life. What's worse, rebirth as an animal or torment in hell could be attained because of bad karma.

According to the teachings and philosophies of the Buddha, there are six realms of existence: the higher realm of the heavens, the human realm, and the four lower realms of torment. The four lower realms are often described as Hell in layman's term. Hell, as we know it, consists of all types of rascals and horrifying elements—beasts, voracious ghosts, demons, and hell monsters. These realms indicate where a soul will go after his death.

The highest realm or state is intended for people who have lived their lives beyond what is in accordance with moral values. They are exceedingly noble and have spent their lives doing good deeds. The second one, or the human realm, is a state where the human soul is considered fortunate since it was reborn again in human form and was allowed to achieve Nirvana or end the rebirth cycle. As for those who chose to live in evilness and cruelty, the last realms of Hell await their souls.

Traditionally, Buddhists believe that even the Enlightened One was not excused from experiencing Karma. There is one renowned story about the Buddha, where one of his cousins attempted to kill him by dropping a large stone on him. The attempt was unsuccessful; however, it caused the Buddha's foot to be injured. The Buddha explained that this resulted from a karmic reprisal for an attempted murder he had planned on doing to his stepbrother back in his earlier life.

If we analyze it, karma is one of the most significant laws that greatly concern the happenings in our life. It is an essential ingredient in one's personal growth. When we live our lives based on what we know, we can reach an understanding of ourselves that others can't take away from us. This is when we are able to experience a great sense of fulfillment and peace.

From an artistic point of view, karma can serve as a law of human nature where one is capable of creating his own reality. We act as though we are artists painting on a canvas, but instead, our bodies, minds, and experiences in life are the mediums of our own life creation.

The objective of Zen Buddhism is for us to avoid the consequences of bad karma. We are cultured to follow Buddha's teachings and principles to help us avoid the occurrence of rebirth. Not necessarily to attain good karma but to be born in a more pleasant state.

Suffering and How to End It

In the Buddha's first sermon as the Enlightened One, he has talked about the *Four Noble Truths,* which expounds the idea of human suffering.

Ancient myths have told that he has come up with this idea upon witnessing four sad events of human existence and non-existence that greatly moved him.

    a.) The suffering of an old man
    b.) The suffering of a sick man
    c.) The death of man
    d.) The modest life of an ascetic (a monk)

It was in these moments that he was able to gather thoughts and deeply ponder on the reality of things in a man's life.

If you notice, the Dharma was overstating the idea of suffering many times, and you may think that Buddhism is just as miserable as it looks. Conversely, the Buddhist community does not view these either as depressing or comforting but fairly, a realistic perspective of natural life. It does not count on the positive side or the negative side but rather on what is actually real.

The idea of suffering does not only refer directly to grief and desolation, but it also acknowledges the existence of happiness and pleasure. However, as realistic as possible, the Dharma depicts happiness and pleasure as somewhat temporary. It only occurs in a short period of time or only during that particular moment.

To understand it better, let us talk about a detailed framework of the concept of suffering. The Four Noble Truths sum up the core of the Dharma. They are the product of the Buddha's awareness and realizations about life and death. Although seemingly vague and difficult to understand, they have endured centuries and were passed down in different interpretations by scholars worldwide.

The Four Noble Truths

First Noble Truth: Dukkha – The Truth of Suffering

The word *Dukkha* is a Pali/Sanskrit word, which means "suffering." According to Buddhist dharmas, the term is defined as "incapable of satisfying" or "not capable of resisting anything." More commonly, it refers to anything temporary or conditional.

The Buddha's first noble truth explains that nothing in the world will make a man contented. Man, in nature, is always hungry and never satisfied, making it the chief cause of all the suffering in this world.

Suffering exists. It is inescapable. The first three events that the Buddha witnessed (man's old age, sickness, and death) are all tantamount to suffering. There is no person on this planet that I have known who is incapable of experiencing distress. Even the richest individual or the luckiest person alive is subject to suffer. We may not know what kind of pain each one of us has to experience, but it is just a matter of time before it comes right before us.

Suffering comes in different ways and forms. It also depends on the gravity of the incident. It can be in the form of depression, emotional pain like anguish or jealousy, or worse, suicide attempts and physical agony.

The first noble truth attests to the underlying consequence of man's existence. We won't find the perfect happiness somewhere else because we are set to struggle in our lives. Life in all its forms is never ideal. In a reflective sense, life doesn't always go the way we expect it to. It is an endless battle to fight for.

Second Noble Truth: Samudaya – The Truth of the Cause of Suffering

In a day-to-day setting where we are involved in disputes and encounter personal problems and issues, it seems easy to recognize the cause of our pain and grief. However, in Buddhism, there is a deeper identified cause of all sufferings, a profound understanding of the root of our difficulties and fears.

The Buddha taught it in his second noble truth, which he described as the Three Roots of Evil, or the Three Fires of Hate. They are as follows:

- **Desire**

The desire to control and acquire things is part of human nature. Man has this unceasing thirst for satisfaction. The second teaching does not tell us that we must surrender everything we have to find real happiness. In that manner, there is a more subtle issue that lies behind it. It is the attachment to the things that we desire that puts us in trouble.

Desires can take several different forms. The most common examples are greed for money, desire for power, craving of carnal pleasure, aspiring to become famous, and even the desire to avoid unwanted happenings such as anxiety, sorrow, jealousy, and rage from happening.

The nature of humans is full of dreams and desires; however, it does not necessarily mean that much of the desires of mankind are destructive and bad. There are also good kinds of desires, such as the desire for peace and enlightenment, though at times someone's pursuit of happiness becomes a craving and, when overlooked later on, turns to greed. This seems to be true at some point in our lives. For instance, we are aware that most people need money to survive, however, others who already have enough want more. These types of people tend to think and do harm unto others for the sake of their wants.

Some people give love and want love in return, yet they could not receive it. Even if it looks like we are asking for the good, the second noble truth teaches us that excessive desire, regardless of the reason, may lead us to peril—or worse, to do evil things.

▪ Ignorance or Delusion

According to the Buddha, the desire initially grows from self-ignorance. We, as human beings, run into our lives chasing things at the same time. We do this for security—to have a sense of confidence about ourselves and the world around us. We tend to get attached not only to material things but also with thoughts, ideas, and opinions concerning ourselves. When this attachment continues, it usually turns to an obsession that makes us exasperated little by little when everything we want does not fall into place. This is where hatred comes in.

- **Hatred**

Consequent to ignorance are feelings of anxiousness built up inside of us. We are filled with a destructive urge, as described in *The Fire Sermon* that the Buddha taught; all is burning. When anger starts to build up in us, whatever we see becomes unpleasant and annoying. And so it goes, that whatever the eyes have seen (eye consciousness and eye contact), be it pleasant, painful, or not painful is burning with the fire of hate, lust, illusion, and anguish.

Third Noble Truth: Nirodha – The Truth of the End of Suffering

In Sanskrit, *Nirodha* means "cessation." To liberate oneself from the chains of attachment is to liberate oneself from suffering. The Buddha became a living example of the third noble truth. He has taught about our possibility of freedom and unveiled the secret to enlightenment.

Unlike the first and second noble truths, which tell us about the darkness of suffering, the third truth gives us hope to look forward to positive things that are yet to come. Moreover, it also tells us that the way out of *dukkha* is to end our attachment and cravings to excessive things.

Nirodha is like telling yourself to stop eating your favorite food. You cannot assure yourself to stop craving from now on just because you've said it. This doesn't work out easily because the conditions you've set for not craving will still exist.

Although it may seem difficult and impossible to cut back on our desires, the Buddha taught us that it is with diligent practice that we can succeed when we are able to see how impermanent everything is and when we can accept that grasping for ephemeral things will never satisfy us is the time that letting go is easier. It is when the craving seems to diminish on its own.

This is the point when we get to experience Nirvana.

Fourth Noble Truth: Magga – The Truth of the Path that Leads to the End of Suffering

Among the noble truths that the Buddha has taught in his forty-five years of sermons, the last one is the most spoken. The majority of the Dharma consists of life teachings about the *Eightfold Path.* In this section, I will talk about the Buddha's cure to suffering—a precept to the end of suffering and how it leads us to enlightenment.

The Eightfold Path, also called the Middle Way, eludes both indulgence and asceticism. Unlike in other religions and philosophies, Buddhism does not centralize the idea of believing in the doctrine alone but by living it and walking the path.

This path touches our day-to-day life in every way. It is a series of lessons and ethical conduct of our everyday activities to mindfulness. Every action, thought, and language is addressed by the Eightfold Path. It serves as a guide towards discipline and reconciliation. Without it, the first three noble truths will remain a theory.

The Eightfold Path

The first two steps of the Eightfold Path constitute a sense of wisdom that is believed to be present in each one of us if only we will open our inner self.

i. Right Understanding (Sammā ditthi)

The Buddha's teachings do not intend to be understood blindly by its followers. It is for them to experience and be able to realize if it were true. The first step is for us to understand that life in its ways is inevitable of human distractions, that we are prone to committing mistakes. Yet, we are called to open our minds and hearts of the truth that lies within. This is a momentous step of the Eightfold Path since it interconnects us to the reality of life. Thus, it stands as a preparation for the journey towards the path. In general, all of the Buddha's teachings are merely for practice. They are not created only as philosophies to be believed in or idolized.

ii. Right Intention (Sammā sankappa)

The second step is where we become faithful to the path. We begin to choose what is right and decide on what is best for us. Basically, Right

Understanding demonstrates to us the naked reality of life, including the problems that revolve in it, while Right Intention guides us to where our heart desires.

The first step of the path marks an upfront discussion in understanding the perspective of suffering, its cause, and how we can end it. Now that we are interested in following the path towards freedom, we should begin to apply the perspective of Right Understanding to the intentions we live by so we can be able to identify and assess if our intentions either cause our suffering or not.

Our intentions are the principal basis of what we will think, say, or do. However, there is a deeper implication behind what we only want. It is more about the motive of why we want what we want. For instance, I am planning to buy a car. The basic intention might be for ease of transportation for myself or my family. It may also be for the intention of showing off to my friends or other people. Frequently, there are several intentions present in a desire; hence, if I solely think that my intention is just to impress, I may not consider other more important purposes of buying the car.

The intentions that we live by are significant in contributing to our mental health. They have a major influence on affecting our personality, psychological welfare, and our lives. When our intentions are motivated with happiness, we establish a habit of conditioning ourselves to greater happiness. To do so, the Buddha involved three Right Thoughts, which contradict the harmful intentions that lead to suffering. These are:

- Renunciation (Nekkhamma) - Nekkhamma, which means renunciation of relinquishment from lust, is a Buddhist practice that opposes the insatiable desires of the flesh. In Buddhism, renunciation is not referred to as something one must do, but it is something that one must understand with wisdom (considering the idea of cause and effect).

- Loving-kindness (Metta) – refers to acts of goodwill and compassion to other people, including oneself. It is the opposite of aversion, loathe, and malevolence.
- Harmlessness (Avyāpāda) – is the absence of the desire to injure. It refers to nonviolence and nonaggression.

Right intent requires a judgment emanated from the heart, a recognition of life's goodwill and fairness. It means having the determination and urge to continue the journey despite the hurdles that might come through.

iii. **Right Speech (Sammā vācā)**

What your mind thinks, your mouth speaks. When someone does something wrong to us, we tend to say foul words out of anger against that person. The quality of our thoughts automatically connects with our way of communicating because we become absorbed by our emotions at that moment.

The aim of the Right Speech is for us to refrain from speaking lies, insults that may cause a revolt, malicious language, and gossip. A rightful mind cannot speak harsh and hurtful speech. We, as Buddhas, must not only speak benevolently but also speak of what is only true. If, for instance, honesty comes with a lash, and it is not that necessary to tell, we just need to remain in "noble silence."

Communicating kindly helps us resolve disputes, unites us to others, and eludes us from living through regrets caused by dissent. By practicing thoughtful communication, we are more likely to come closer to living a compassionate life.

iv. **Right Action (Sammā kammanta)**

Right Action aims to promote only what is right, more particularly peace and harmony. In the sermon of the Buddha, he enumerated five immoral acts that we must abstain from: killing, stealing, telling lies, sexual transgression, and addiction to drugs and intoxicants. We are obliged to act in accordance with the moral teachings.

Aside from the aforementioned, we as human beings can distinguish what is right and what is wrong, and what can and what cannot harm others. Thus, it is our responsibility to spare any kind of action that is against the moral teachings.

v. **Right Livelihood (Sammā ājīva)**

Right Livelihood and Right Action work hand in hand. In order to progress towards the spiritual path, man must not only watch his actions but on his source of living as well.

Right Livelihood means that you should withdraw any type of livelihood which causes harm to human beings or animals. Such examples are: work that deals with weapons, liquors, intoxicants, poisons, gun shops, and the like. Slave trade is also discouraged since it deals with human abuse, astrology, and fortune-telling belief is also prohibited since it relies on a fixed future. The Buddha does not encourage certain types of work like these, which he detailed during his sermon.

The last three steps mentioned above (Right Speech, Right Action, and Right Livelihood) are related and constituted to establish moral ethics. Buddhism aims to promote peace and harmony both individually and as a community. This moral conduct serves as the basis of all divine accomplishments. Thus, without them, spiritual development would be impossible.

vi. **Right Effort (Sammā vāyāma)**

Right Effort, as described in the Eightfold Path, is a positive and balanced attitude towards our actions and decisions. It aims to prevent unwholesome behaviors that might cause evil to arise.

It is an energetic will that promotes optimism, promoting the mind to think of only positive, clear, and honest thoughts. Our minds are wholesome by nature, and the objective of this path is to trigger our thoughts to focus only on the positive things and drop down any form of negativity. Right Effort requires determination and thorough concentration to be fully achieved.

vii. **Right Mindfulness (Sammā sati)**

In line with exerting great effort towards our thinking, Right Mindfulness guides us to be fully aware and observant of our movements, thoughts, feelings, and ideas. Right Mindfulness asks us to be mindful of the moment; to focus on what is there at present.

When we go to a place, we see different elements—people, animals, buildings, trees. We hear noises—the sound of people chattering, the chirping of the birds, cars passing. We also feel the atmosphere of the place. This is the kind of moment that we have to focus on, not thinking of what will happen next and what we have left behind.

Right Mindfulness does not tell us to exclude our thoughts to the reality existing ahead of us. Thus, it helps us meditate and contemplate the goodness of the present moment. At this moment, we can control our habits and upcoming actions, including our fear.

Listening to a favorite song makes us forget all our worries. It makes us enjoy the moment while it is being played. At times, it puts us in a lighter mood not only when we listen to it, but even after we played it. Essentially, it helps shape our disposition and attitude towards the activities of our daily lives.

This is an example of what the Buddha is telling us. Be it in the form of art, music, a sport, or a hobby, we are all called to always live in the moment.

Have you lived your moment recently?

viii. **Right Concentration (Sammā samādhi)**

Right Concentration and Right Mindfulness may have a similar objective when it comes to focus. Both teach the mind to see and appreciate things in the moment as they are. Distinctively, the Right Concentration of the mind is a mental discipline where our minds are taught to select thoughts worthy of our well-being. Not everything that we see, hear, and feel must be welcomed; thus, we only need to concentrate on what may be valuable to us in our journey towards the path.

The last aspect of the Eightfold Path leads us to the four stages of *Dhyana.* The four *Dhyanas,* or most commonly called the Absorptions in the English language, allows us to experience the essence of the Buddha's teachings directly. They serve as our entrance to enter the state of Nirvana.

The Stages of Dhyana

1. Before experiencing the *Dhyanas*, one must be able to conquer the five hindrances in Buddhism— sensory desire, ill will, sloth and torpor, restlessness and worry, and doubt. Each of these must be replaced with happy and healthy thoughts for the mind. This is the first stage of the Dhyana.

2. In the second stage, the mind is slowly becoming inactive. There is a feeling of calmness and one-pointedness (Ekaggatā) in the mind. The sense of euphoria in the first stage is still present.

3. In the third stage, equanimity (Upeksā) resides. The feeling of euphoria leaves the body. There is real mental calmness and clarity.

4. In the fourth and last stage, the sensory abilities stop. The state of mind and soul seem to separate from the physical body.

Equanimity is the only thing that remains.

Achieving Nirvana

Yes, you've probably heard of Nirvana in other places. The word is so pervasive that its real implication is a lot of times mislaid. Legendarily, the term Nirvana was used by a famous grunge band in America in reference to their actual band name. The meaning of Nirvana is so impeccable that it was personally picked by the band's frontman, Kurt Cobain, in honor of the Buddhist philosophy.

But what does Nirvana really mean?

Nirvana, in Sanskrit, means "to extinguish" or "to blow out." In the spiritual definition of Buddhism, the ones being extinguished are the fires of evil where hate, greed, and lust instigate. As discussed in the previous context, the Buddha enumerated and expounded in detail the Eightfold Path that guides us towards experiencing Nirvana. The eradicated fires must be transformed with deep reconciliation and peace. In a simpler sense, Nirvana is achieved when suffering (hate, greed, and lust) and rebirth are ended.

Other non-Buddhist traditions and philosophies, like in Hinduism, where it is defined as a rebirth of karmic predispositions, have a different interpretation of the term Nirvana. However, the most widely known Buddhist perspective is where the Buddha has exhibited living proof of enlightenment.

According to Buddha, Nirvana is the highest state one can reach. As he defined, one can achieve it at the end of life or in the course of existence.

We must understand that Nirvana is not a place but rather a state of existence. Although labeled as such, the Buddha warns us that whatever we say or conceive of Nirvana would be wrong. A state of perfection could never be described into words alone, especially in an ordinary survival setting. Therefore, it is beyond reason. There is no scientific explanation that can better define the state of Nirvana. It is beyond space and time, and it is a state that can only be experienced.

Through the years, there have been different analyses as to how the Buddha's teachings were addressed. In other scriptures, some people believe that we can enter a place called Nirvana, just like we enter a room in a house. Other beliefs came from the Mahayana sutras, where it was believed that only individuals who are reborn as men are allowed to enter Nirvana. Yet, it was refuted by the Vimalakirti Sutra, defending that all genders, male and female, all social status, and the laypeople are entitled to become enlightened.

Reincarnation

Do you ever wonder why some things seem to have already happened to you? A place or a person looks familiar, or you felt that you used to be someone else?

In several native regions, the belief of having to live more than one life is normal. It is a belief that when a person dies, his or her soul goes out through the nostrils and the mouth, leaving the physical body. The soul then transfers to another body either in the form of a human, animal, or an insect. The belief goes that the rebirth of the person depends on how he or she has lived his or her life in the past.

In Southern Africa, there is this idea that after death, the soul of the person stays near the grave where its dead body was buried for a short period of time. Once it has reached a certain number of days, it will then find another dwelling place or another human body where it will reside.

In other parts of the world, reincarnation is mostly considered in Asian religions. Most especially in India, where Buddhism, Jainism, Hinduism, and Sikhism are all practiced. One thing they have in common is the role of karma in reincarnation.

There are many stories and testimonies from people worldwide as to how they believed to have experienced reincarnation. In many different cases, it was found that such experiences occur most likely in children ages two to six years old.

I remember reading a story from one of my father's books about a young girl who was believed to have reincarnated. It happened the night when she was asleep; she began to mumble unfamiliar words loudly and quickly awakened her parents.

They recognized that she was speaking in the French language, which was strange, knowing that neither spoke French nor had gone outside of the country. The parents of the young girl only knew a little of the language, which gave them a hard time understanding what she was saying. This left them with no choice but to record it.

The young girl was six years of age and had never been exposed to someone who spoke French. Confused, the parents went to a French teacher of a resident high school who could translate the recording. They found out that the girl on the tape was looking for her mother, who seemed to have been missing after the Germans attacked their community. The parents never believed in reincarnation, but the facts given were really unexplainable.

Based on science, the occurrence of speaking a foreign language, which was not purposely learned, among children and adults is uncommon but possible. According to Dr. Charles Richet, a well-known French physiologist and parapsychologist and a recipient of the Nobel prize, there is still a likelihood for such events. This finding was called "Xenoglossy," a term he had coined.

However, for a person of a categorically young age who has limited knowledge and experience, it is quite convincing to consider paranormal explanations with which is reincarnation.

Key Points

- All human beings are Buddhas
- Each person is invited to live a life of Enlightenment
- Suffering exists, and it is an inexorable aspect of life
- The Four Noble Truths explains how suffering is relevant in our life:
    - The Truth of Suffering
    - The Truth of the Cause of Suffering
    - The Truth of the End of Suffering
    - The Truth the Path that leads to the End of Suffering
- The Eightfold Path is eight practices created by Buddha that, when followed, guides us to the path towards enlightenment
- Karma is the result of one's actions in his previous life; it primarily dictates the fate of a person's life in his future existence
- Nirvana is the supreme form of state that one can attain

- Reincarnation is the rebirth of one's soul to a new life after death

CHAPTER THREE

Zen Buddhism: Benefits and Techniques

"Do not let the behavior of others destroy your inner peace."

- *Dalai Lama*

I remember it was a Sunday night in September. I went to a fancy party, where a former colleague from work invited me. I was sitting at a table with other individuals when I met this middle-aged lady I thought was sort of familiar to me. Turns out, I've met her once on a writers' conference way back when I was starting my writing career. I recognized her because she did a talk about Zen Buddhism and how it helped her survive depression.

Ever since, I was always curious about spiritual techniques and philosophical practices. I wondered how they worked and how they affected people's lives. Being passionate about fitness was my way out of the constant hassle and stress of everyday life. I'd tried various activities, including yoga, but I hadn't tried Zen meditation yet. And so I've decided to learn and hopefully master it.

One of the best techniques to practice Buddhism is through meditation. Basically, when we talk about meditations, they often provide us with relaxation and stress relief. It is a given advantage that most forms of meditation provide. But unlike others, Zen Buddhism offers a more profound intention that sets both the human body and soul in harmony. As discussed in the other chapters of this book, the practice of Zen meditation instills in us the values of mindfulness and inner peace. But what is more, is how it can benefit us on a long-term basis.

The main benefit Zen meditation gives in the Buddhist tradition is its ability to provide awareness on how the mind works. Honestly, my first Zen journey was challenging due to numerous factors. When I first tried it, I found it hard to focus, maybe because I was used to the hustle and bustle of the city life.

First Stage

As expected, just like any other day, my schedule was jam-packed with projects, assignments, and commitments that I had yet to accomplish. I had no time or good reason at all to start it, but opportunity knocked. I was given a task where I was assigned to do a short journal article about meditations, so I did it anyway.

I performed my first Zen meditation in my old apartment. I did not have a meditating space, so I just used an exercise mat where I could sit comfortably and placed it beside my bed next to the window, hoping to get a peaceful vibe out of my makeshift meditation space.

It was nearly five in the morning; I chose to listen to an online meditation podcast just like any beginner would. I followed every step earnestly with the best of my abilities, but whenever I close my eyes, my mind becomes active and restless. I couldn't seem to calm my thoughts.

I sat down for a few minutes and tried hard to shut off my mind, but I couldn't. I was totally annoyed with myself for being so cranky. What I was expecting to bring peace to my mind was an absolute opposite. The more I forced my mind to relax, the more thoughts that popped into it.

I also found it hard to turn off e-mail notifications and calls because I was worried that my boss might need me while I was on the verge of my meditating session, and at the same time, I was used to checking my social media accounts. This was the first obstacle I encountered in my first effort to try Zen meditation.

I started doubting if I had what it took to be a Zen person. Hence, after evaluating my experience, I opted to do research and found an inspiring piece from a book where the author emphasized the wrong ideas of Zen meditations. The reality is that we cannot stop our thoughts; we can let them pass by. Zen meditation helps us to be aware of our thoughts without using judgment.

After an enlightening discernment, I have come to realize that it was right and possible. In my attempts to try Zen meditation, I have come up with a few realizations about how it would be best to perform it, especially for beginners.

- Make sure that you are prepared both physically and mentally
- Do not rush; take the time to condition yourself
- Not required, but you may want to allocate space for your meditation

- Try to research and have a background about Zen and its techniques
- Turn off devices and gadgets that could distract you

Second Stage

Through consistent practice, I was able to perform it successfully. I didn't notice it until I finished the session, and I saw that thirty minutes had already passed without interruptions. During the experience, I felt lightness and peace. I felt like I was very light, like that of a feather. There were complete serenity and calmness. The effect to me was somehow hypnotic, and I became sleepier than before. As guaranteed, the effect of Zen meditation was really promising. Evidently, one of its main benefits is relaxation. In science, good breathing relaxation increases the body's oxygen level, which conditions both the mind and the body to function less. In effect, sleeping is much easier and better.

In my attempts to continue with what I started, I switched up my morning sessions to an evening schedule before going to bed. It made my sleeping pattern easier because I was able to sleep immediately after each sitting. It was also surprising because my gadget dependency lessened. I can say that the experience was extraordinary and worthwhile. It improved my day-to-day life and reduced my levels of stress and anxiety.

Third Stage

At this point, I was able to practice it consistently. I made it a point to perform it every week before I go to bed for thirty minutes to an hour or depending on how flexible my schedule was. Practicing Zen was a commitment and, at the same time, an investment. It significantly changed my life for the better, and I become more appreciative of its essence.

On a personal note, Zen taught me a lot of things and helped improve my well-being. It worked wonders in my sleeping pattern and with my way of thinking.

1. **It improved my focus and memory**
    Of all Zen's benefits, the most recognizable is its ability to improve focus and concentration. As stated in various

studies, stress causes a lot of issues and problems, including mental function. It directly impacts memory and even intensifies mental illness. When a person is stressed, his memory tends to slow down, and the ability of the mind to focus and retain information is impeded.

In my case, I was able to accomplish my assignments and projects ahead of time. My usual distractions no longer distracted me because my attention span had improved, and I even had extra time for my sports and other hobbies. Having a retentive memory and a healthy mindset helped me to easily finish my tasks. Also, it kept me away from unwanted diversions that might distract me.

2. It boosted my mood and confidence

Ever since I performed my Zen sessions, I started going to bed earlier and more comfortably. As we all know, getting the right amount of sleep helps improve our moods. Thus, a positive mood leads to a positive way of thinking.

In my fifth week of Zen meditation, one of my bosses suddenly commended me at work for successfully accomplishing a project at that time. I didn't realize that I was becoming highly energetic and more motivated at work, not until that moment. Since then, I started becoming more confident in myself, and that continued throughout my Zen journey.

3. **It enhanced my creativity**

Before, I was only into sports and writing. I didn't have much of a hobby until I became interested in music. I think it started when I listened to mellow tracks during meditation. Of all the different genres of music that I have explored, the most remarkable one that fascinated me was classical music. The relaxing and peaceful feeling it gives is what I loved the most about it.

With great fondness for music, I watched online tutorials on how to play the piano whenever I have the time. Truly, Zen meditation opened me to more opportunities to enhance my creativity.

4. It boosted my energy levels

According to a study at the University of Waterloo, practicing quick sessions of mindful meditation with Hatha yoga involved at least twenty minutes a day can remarkably increase brain function and energy levels. Meditation is a form of relaxation that allows our bodies and minds to relax, providing us with better sleep and a good energy level.

Hatha yoga and mindfulness meditation are two effective practices that allow our minds to limit the processing of unnecessary information so that our energy can be reserved for other activities.

As time has gone by, I have found more ways of practicing Zen meditation. Actually, there are a number of casual techniques on how to apply Zen in our everyday lives. Beyond sitting in meditation, we can also achieve stillness while walking, drinking our coffee, or even while doing our routines.

Zen meditation has a lot of methods that we often doubt and overlook. The most common misconceptions involve its contemplation style and setting. A lot of times, we think we must climb mountains, shave our heads, and be like a monk in order to succeed in it, but in fact, it doesn't really matter.

Regardless of who we are and where we came from, anyone can follow the path of Zen and do well. There are no right or wrong ways of doing Zen. Whether formal or informal, its effectiveness depends on how we perceive and believe it.

The essence of Zen Buddhism inspires us to seek peace and satisfaction from within ourselves. It does not conform to what is common, just like other meditational practices that only provide fleeting benefits. Zen Buddhism's principle emphasizes that we can only attain true harmony through continuous experience and not rely on its idea per se.

As ironic as it might seem, the Zen meditation technique works best when we are busy. This is because it is the time when we need peace and quiet the most. There is an old Zen saying that goes like this: "You should sit in meditation for 20 minutes a day. Unless you're too busy, then you should sit for an hour."

For beginners, you can start meditating for at least five minutes each day. You may start by taking slow deep breaths, listening to soft background music or your surroundings, or just barely looking up to the sky. Take time to enjoy the moment without doing or thinking of anything. You will be surprised that after doing this, your mood has significantly improved. Undeniably, a few minutes of silence is essential to clear our minds from constant noise and stress.

Day by day, increase your time to ten minutes or more until you reach the standard thirty-minute meditation. It is recommended that you find time to do this no matter how busy you are because the effects are worthy in the long run.

Zen meditation techniques can regulate our emotions and mental inclination. When our minds are clear and stable at all times, our thoughts and attitude towards the things around us become more positive. It becomes noticeable in us that we are slowly recreating a better version of ourselves. Hence, the core of Buddhism progressively affects us.

Buddhism is known to be concerned about open-handedness, as it teaches "the more that you give to others, the more you will receive." The concept implies a stylistic expression of how generosity offers us a larger threshold of opportunities. When we are selfless, we do not expect anything in return, which makes us free from imminent distress caused by too many expectations. Thus, people are more than willing to help us if we need help in the future. This goes back to the concept of Karma. Relative to the cause and effect of things, we attract positivity when we live our lives positively; what we do unto others comes back to us in a different form but with the same gravity.

In a common context, Zen practice often encourages us to live a life of compassion and simplicity to avoid unwanted things from happening. According to a Zen master, when we seek inner peace, the more it would be difficult to find it. Hence, when we do not ask for any reward despite extending help, and when we choose other's happiness instead of ourselves, there is a greater possibility of attaining peace.

We learn from this idea that unlike other meditations that provide short-term solutions to life problems, Zen is focused on addressing the main issue, the core of the problem. It delves into a more serious issue that helps improve not only our physical well-being but also our spiritual identity.

The way to achieve peace and openness is not complicated as it seems to be. It is simple, yet requires a thorough effort to understand. Beneficially, when one attains the Zen technique, there will be remarkable changes in a person's life. You do not necessarily need to be a Zen master to prove that it is effective for you. Whether you enrolled in a meditation class or you just learned it by yourself, the effects will reflect in time.

Truly, the Zen technique of Buddhism serves as a medium of self-discovery and self-improvement that is morally upright. In addition, it encourages its followers to become appreciative of everything we have, even in the slightest form. When we look at everything with gratitude, we are able to obtain a sense of happiness within ourselves for the reason that we do not allow pessimism to lead our lives.

Takeaway Points

- Zen Buddhism can help you become a more positive and appreciative person.

- The essence of Zen Buddhism is to seek peace and satisfaction within oneself.
- One can only attain true harmony by continuously practicing the principles of Zen Buddhism and not merely fixating on its ideologies.
- Zen Buddhism can lean you towards the path of self-discovery and self-improvement.

CHAPTER FOUR
Buddhism and Mindfulness

"Mindfulness is a way
Of befriending ourselves
And our experience."
-Jon Kabat – Zinn

In our modern world, the mindfulness technique has inevitably gained a reputation in terms of the psychological help it has given to people. There are previous findings that mental rehabilitation based on mindfulness has been effective in preventing the recurrence of depression and anxiety.

In certain mental and psychological institutions, there are proven cases where individuals who suffer from mental illnesses and anxiety disorders have claimed that their perspective of life has improved. Nevertheless, it would be more preferable to say that the technique did not solve their conditions, but it helped alleviate their symptoms.

In other areas, mindfulness is a state of mind; for others, it is a practice. But according to the Buddhist teacher Joseph Goldstein, mindfulness is "the quality and power of mind that is aware of what is happening, without judgment and without interference."

Mindfulness is about cultivating. It aims to create awareness of thoughts and emotions in our surroundings without using judgment. It is a technique adapted from Buddhism to aid us in our typical day to day problems. Palpably, the mindfulness technique instituted an effective system of addressing mental health issues.

Even though there are studies that show how effective it is in providing psycho-biological effects in reducing anxiety, there is no clear explanation as to how it works. Mindfulness and meditation are two important aspects of the success of mindfulness-based mental therapy. Some people have claimed success from the therapies, but for others, it did not work.

Considering that the practice of mindful meditation has brought positive effects to certain individuals because it is indeed harmless and easy to follow, there are also quite a number of downsides. While meditation often leads its practitioners to enlightenment, others are able to resurface negative thoughts and emotions during the sessions. Often, this happens to people who have experienced a traumatic past. Thus, we must remember that the Buddhist mindfulness was not created to serve as a medication to heal us or to give happiness in our life. It is a practice that seeks beyond what is common to our needs. It is a more profound understanding of how we live our lives in a better way.

In different ideologies, the efficacy of mindfulness only depends on how the person handles the circumstances. When practiced carefully and morally, it reduces suffering. Also, when we apply it in our everyday life, we can follow the Dharma teachings. According to the Buddha, the goal of mindfulness is to end suffering. That is why he established the Eightfold Path for us to be guided on how to practice mindfulness effectively.

As the Buddha continued on his sermons, he gave responsibility to his senior monk Bhikkhus, to educate their students about the Four Foundations of Mindfulness.

The Four Foundations of Mindfulness

- ## *Mindfulness of the Body*

Practicing the mindfulness of the body means that you should look at "the body inside the body," meaning to say, the Buddha wants us to recognize that our bodies are not unified or barely compact. The body consists of different small parts that are individually formed. It comprises the brain, heart, lungs, teeth, bones, eyes, etc. Each "body" portion is positioned in a much wider body.

Through this, the Buddha teaches us that the composition of body parts represents a physical form that comes into existence, which only endures in a specific amount of time. The human body is inclined to experience injury, disease, and, eventually, death. Our lives are temporary—so is our happiness. Since our bodies are not permanent, then we can say that our bodies are not ours to keep. Thus, we must distinguish "the body as it really is," as stated by the Buddha.

- ### *Mindfulness of Feelings*

  Similar to how the Buddha wants us to realize the mindfulness of the body, the practice of mindfulness of feelings is to realize that there is a "feeling in the feeling." Our feelings or emotions comprise of subdivided feelings which are activated at a particular moment when are sensation is stimulated. These are pleasant feelings, unpleasant feelings, and neutral feelings.

  When we are feeling happy, the pleasant feeling is activated. Therefore, neither the unpleasant nor the neutral feeling is present then. This happens the same thing when we are sad or in a neutral state. There is only one feeling currently triggered, and the other two are inactive.

  We are taught to view our feeling this way for us to recognize our feelings as only a part of a bigger emotion. As that particular feeling arises, we notice that feelings are somehow temporary. When we are delighted, it looks like it only lasts for quite a while, but when we are angry, it seems like we have been angry forever.

This is the reason why we know feelings could be disappointing sometimes. Due to this, the Buddha calls us to recognize "feelings as they are" and that we are not subject to it.

- ***Mindfulness of the Mind***
Looking through our minds, we might think that the mind is a distinct state. Hence, the mind is just a progression of another mind, which is vaster. The information is sent to our brains once our senses are prompted at the moment. Our consciousness covers a wide range of senses, which are, as we all know, the sense of sight, hearing, smell, taste, and touch. These five main senses are significant in the processing of our internal intellectual state. The mind is such a powerful space that we can stock up on millions of dreams, thoughts, ideas, and memories in it.

  Though, if you will observe, the mind only depends on internal and external factors. It isn't permanent, and it could change from one minute to another. Every feeling passes by in a glimpse. It comes, stays for a while, and goes away eventually. For this reason, we are taught to understand that we are not our thoughts, and we could not be defined based on our thoughts alone. The mind is a channel of constant impermanence. As the Buddha teaches, we should look at the "mind as it really is."

- ### *Mindfulness of the Phenomena or the Dhammas*

  The Buddha always teaches us about the context of the dhammas, that we must not only learn it as it is but to understand it more deeply. Naturally, the human being was born with an endless curiosity, and the Buddha supports this, but only what is true and moral. He, too, was ambitious to seek the truth about life, so he did everything to succeed.

  Out of inquisitiveness, he continued his pursuit of the truth in almost everything and even sought the maker, our source of existence. This is where he discovered that no one else and nothing in this world could gratify him. Hence, he was able to discover a more significant point. He found out that man is subject to experience such phenomena in life. Man must undergo birth, growth, aging, pain, illness, and death, all of which are inevitable to mankind, to understand the essence of one's life. The Buddha learned that it is not only a problem that he must battle alone but of each human being. Accordingly, he searched for answers within himself and found enlightenment.

The Four Foundations of Mindfulness are the key things that we should be mindful of. They are intended for us to see things as how they really are, far from our conjectural ideas of them. As a result, we are able to see reality and truth more transparently.

According to Buddhism, there is nothing wrong with human beings. The problem exists because we are not able to understand the nature of reality. Thus, the Buddha aims to help us develop our responsiveness towards reality by providing ways to practice mindfulness.

To help you get started, here is a step by step guide of Applying Mindfulness through

Meditation that you can easily follow anytime anywhere:

1. Allocate a quiet space or a room where you can freely perform your meditation. You may want to make sure that the place is peaceful and comfortable. Sit on the floor with your legs crossed, similar to a "full lotus" meditating position. If you find yourself uncomfortable in this position, sit straight on a chair without leaning at your back and stretch your legs with your feet flat on the floor.

2. Place your hands on your lap, as if touching each of your thighs. Maintain a good posture while sitting and ensure that you are not slouching. Look forward and keep your chin up.

3. Relax your posture and keep your shoulder blades engaged to avoid tension. Your lower body must feel the weight, and the upper part must feel lighter.

4. Do not close your eyes entirely. Allow your eyes to gaze comfortably on what's in front of you. Do this for a minute, then slowly look downwards about five feet in front of you.

5. Focus on your breathing pattern. In this state, you are still aware of what's going on around you. Take time to absorb the moment then slowly, listen to yourself as you inhale the air and exhale it through your mouth and nostrils. After each breath, envision yourself being released together with the air.

6. Whenever you feel that you are getting distracted, say the word "Zen" and focus again on your breathing. At this instance, any form of thought, idea, or emotion that could cause interruption of the meditation must be disregarded immediately by means of referring to the term "Zen."

7. Do this until you feel relaxed and refreshed. At the end of the session, you must be able to set simplicity, calmness, and mindfulness in yourself throughout the day.

These techniques seem very easy if you would just barely theorize them, but in point of fact, it takes a lot of practice to prove its efficacy. The application itself requires seriousness and takes time and effort to perform it successfully.

As mentioned earlier in this chapter, the effect of mindfulness on various individuals is visibly manifested in the modern psychological foundations today. According to Professor Jon Kabat-Zinn, mindfulness practice can be brought and integrated into conventional medicine to improve physical and emotional symptoms among patients. He also believed that the practice could show progress in the behavior, attitude, and mental health of certain people suffering from cognitive and emotional illnesses.

Stress happens to anyone, regardless of age, gender, time, and status. It is a normal part of life; however, it may not be the same for everyone. Dealing with stress depends on a person's way of responding to it. What is stressful for me may not be stressful for you, and vice versa. Thus, the skill of mindfulness is intended for those who experience high levels of stress for them to handle it with ease.

Several studies today have been carrying out research involving children and students since they are more willing to participate than adults. Results show that stress has become common not only to adults and to the workforce but also children and teens. The good news is how mindfulness can benefit persons of all ages without causing harm or risks. Mindfulness techniques are safe and enjoyable. They are proven to provide comfort and ease to beginners and long-time Zen practitioners.

Students, especially teens and young adults, are prone to stress due to sleepless nights, pressure, influence, etc., which lead them to alcoholism and drug abuse. Thus, mindfulness meditation can be taught as early as now for them to be prepared at a young age. In one of the studies from the *Journal of American College Health,* four hundred college women who practiced mindfulness were found to have better physical health, healthier eating habits, and improved sleeping patterns than students who did not undergo the practice.

If you will recall in the previous chapters, one of the benefits of Zen meditations is its ability to control our emotions and way of thinking. Thus, numerous findings support how mindfulness is effective in fighting stress.

Stress reduction programs and exercises are mindfulness platforms that involve thousands of practitioners and experts to administer the programs to identified sufferers. Through these specific courses, symptoms of stress, such as a constant feeling of irritability, restlessness, headaches, lack of energy, etc., are alleviated.

The mindfulness technique teaches a breathing pattern that stimulates our senses to relax. With this, we are able to reap the benefits of lowered anxiety levels, blood pressure, heart rate, and even enhanced our ability to deal with certain illnesses.

The Benefits of Mindfulness to the Young and Old

1. Reduces stress and anxiety
2. Improves physical and mental health
3. Reduces risk of depression
4. Improves academic performance
5. Reduces psychological distress
6. Promotes confidence and boosts self-esteem
7. Boosts creativity and tolerance to stress
8. Improves sleep
9. Increases attention span and focus
10. Develops patience and calmness amidst difficulties

Key Points

- Mindfulness can both be a practice and a state of mind.
- Mindfulness can help you get a grasp of reality.
- Stress, worries, and anxieties can affect anyone, regardless of age, gender, and status. They can have severe implications for life. Nevertheless, they can be managed by practicing mindfulness.
- There are a variety of benefits you can get from practicing mindfulness. Likewise,

there are numerous programs and exercises that you can try to practice it.

- The foundations of mindfulness are meant for you to understand what things really are rather than believing in your own concepts of them.

CHAPTER FIVE

Experiencing Zen in our Everyday Life

"Knowledge is learning something every day.

Wisdom is letting go of something every day."

-Zen Proverb

The practice of Zen Buddhism or Zen does not merely revolve around meditation. It can also be applied to various aspects of our everyday life. Surely, we are all set to experience day to day problems, and the teachings of the Buddha are created to guide us towards a more tranquil and stress-free life.

In our modern world today, numerous distractions tend to disengage us from ourselves and to others. The world is evolving too fast that sometimes we aren't able to get along with it. Hence, the teachings of Buddhism serve as a guide for us to remember how to cope with life.

Buddhism teaches us to learn the art of focus and concentration when we are experiencing confusion. Every day, we are using gadgets and computers to aid us in our work and personal business, and we tend to unconsciously lose our attention to the more important things in our life.

We are so out of focus that we forget to live in the moment. Zen Buddhism not only entails us to practice meditation alone but to bring those learnings in our day to day existence even if our life seems to be full of the hustle and bustle.

One thing about the beauty of Zen is its view of the plainness and tranquillity of everything around us. Seeing a flower, breathing fresh air, or even taking a sip of our favorite coffee, these are the simple things which are common in our everyday lives that we often overlook and forget to enjoy.

Living a life full of earthly possessions, we, at times, get too attached to material objects. This is where the Buddha's teachings come along. Being awakened to the ephemerality of things leads us to acceptance and non-attachment to temporary things, evading us from experiencing suffering. When we do that, we can value more the simplest acts of life, realizing that they are worth living for. Life then is lived in harmony with the body and soul.

What do we do when we are hungry? We feed ourselves to nourish and satisfy our hunger to keep going. Apart from this, it is indeed essential to feed one's soul to see how beautiful life can be. It is not only physically that we live, but by being spiritually full, that makes us truly alive.

When we learn to value simply what is there, we began to see the beauty in everything. Look around and see that all of what exists is made beautifully and uniquely. Unity and harmony invite us to get closer not only to others in the community but also with nature, thus, developing a sense of connection to everything that surrounds us. With this, we are able to manifest in us the values obtained from the Buddha.

One of my favorite sayings that I have followed and lived by personally is an aphorism stated by a monk, Shunryu Suzuki. It goes like this, "Zen is not some kind of excitement, but concentration on our usual everyday routine." Truly, to experience Zen requires more than a feeling. It involves thorough concentration to be fully achieved.

In my everyday life, I always find time to pause for a while from the chaos of the modern world. Taking a short break for oneself is not a sign of unproductivity and selfishness but a useful means to keep going through life. When we begin to discover how to find peace out of conflict and order out of chaos, it is easier to battle our day to day problems.

To help you have a more meaningful life, here are some tips and tricks that might help you find more Zen amidst the confusion.

Zen at Home

1. **Take one step at a time**

    This is a rule that is common to many but rarely followed. Often, we are always in a rush to finish things that we think of doing them at the same time is the best way. Well, multi-tasking could work for others, but to Zen seekers, it may not always be the best way. Multi-tasking tends to cause confusion. Instead, do things one at a time.

List down all that needs to be done and take note of what should be accomplished first. In this way, you are able to do things in order and with accuracy. Watching while eating, playing games while doing an assignment, talking while working; these are some examples of day to day activities that could be improved if you are seeking Zen. When you eat, finish it first. When you work, focus on it alone.

2. Allot a quiet hour

Sometimes allowing yourself to be alone is a sign of a healthy desire—a desire for peace. It does not technically mean being selfish but more of listening to yourself to discover your inner peace. Finding some quiet hour for yourself can be healthy both physically and mentally. After all the tiring and loud noises that we hear every day, our ears deserve to relax. It is also with silence that we can hear what might be going wrong or what the situation calls for. When we acquire these, we become rationally stronger.

Before going to bed, you may want to set your alarm one hour earlier than your actual waking time. In this way, you can meditate, gather your thoughts on what plans you have for the day, write down on your journal, or even perform some exercise. The quiet hour is all yours to take, and you can do whatever you want at that time with peace.

3. Close your eyes and breathe

Sometimes when we are full of things to do and do not know where to start, it is much better to just close our eyes, breathe, and relax our minds. This may not look effective but believe me, it is a good starter for relaxation. Closing your eyes is like shutting off the world for a while to relieve your stress. Thus, it also lets us recognize the beauty of the stillness inside us.

Close your eyes. Calm your thoughts and allow your mind to wander. Listen to your surroundings, and try not to think of anything that may disrupt your meditation. Slowly, take deep breaths at a time. Feel the air going through your nostrils and going inside of your body. Exhale all the negative aura and inhale as if you are breathing the freshest air in the world. Focusing on each breath, you will find yourself slowly getting back to your senses.

4. Consider productive habits as meditation

Meditation is a practice in which you are putting your complete focus on something. It is a means to achieve serenity and composure amidst all complications and confusions. One misconception about meditation is that it is only effective when one sits still and closes his or her eyes. This is the most identified form of meditation; however, there are also a lot of ways to practice it. Cooking, washing the laundry, and cleaning are examples of productive habits that you can consider as a form of meditation.

How?

Focus on each chore. If you are cooking, put your entire attention to it. Do not multi-task, or you may end up burning it or ruining it. Concentrate on making a delicious meal and do it slowly and passionately. You will see, food tastes better when prepared with full attention. Same as through with other chores, finish them one step at a time to achieve better outcomes.

The concept of Zen is not only about immovability but also about focus. When you practice meditation in your everyday activities, you would eventually make it a routine and get used to it; hence, even the most hated chore won't be a burden to you the next time you do it.

5. **Learn to disconnect when necessary**
   Take a period where you don't need to answer phone calls, respond to e-mails, or check social media accounts. It is essential to build healthy boundaries from time to time. Being connected at all times will only cause constant stress due to the continuous flow of information coming in. In instances like this, you are more prone to irritability and a bad temper. Give yourself a break from the busy world.

Turn your cellphones and computers off for a while so you can allow your mind to rest.

Technological advances like the internet and the evolution of social media both have advantages and disadvantages. They serve as a means of communication and news update. However, some studies have shown how frequent checking of social media accounts like Facebook, Twitter, and Instagram may affect a person psychologically and emotionally. Looking at other people's lives and status may trigger envy and a desire to acquire what your neighbor has. So, to avoid these occurrences, concentrate on improving yourself instead of comparing yourself to others.

Aside from disconnecting from these technological devices, it is also fine to disconnect from the people around you. It does not mean that you will cut people off from your life. What you would do is to just focus on yourself and stop checking on other people.

6. Live a simple life

If you observe the life of monks and other followers of Buddhism, they are all living a humble life. They use what is only essential for them. The definition of essential to each human person is different; what may be essential for me may not be essential to you and vice versa. The essence of living simply is for us to appreciate even the smallest type of things. Being appreciative of things spares us from the shadows of greed and discontentment.

Try to get rid of anything unnecessary, especially material things. Separate your needs from your wants to help you identify what you will keep and neglect. What is essential for me is my writing equipment, reading materials, and exercise apparatus. I can live without other things except for these that I have mentioned. As for others, they might not need reading materials; instead, they might need art materials or cooking supplies. There is no specific rule that states what you must and must not have. It depends upon the person's needs.

However, you must always consider what is really important in your life and focus on it by removing the less important things.

7. Find time to be silly

Zen is all about finding peace and happiness. It is not bad to be silly sometimes. After all, we live in order to be happy. Life is not all about study and work. Do not forget to laugh and smile once in a while. As we grow older each day, we tend to lessen telling jokes and silly things. Try to make the most out of your day, for tomorrow it may not be the same.

Laugh while you can and smile often. Sing in the shower while taking a bath, dance while preparing your breakfast, talk to your plants and pets. These are just some of the small things that you can do to make yourself smile for a while. Find time to do what you love, even just for a minute. You will see a big difference in the way you perceive and do things.

8. Practice a healthy lifestyle

When was the last time you had a good run or an exercise that made you sweat? Have you been sleeping enough for the past weeks?

At times, when our schedules are full and hectic, we don't notice anymore how unhealthy we have become. Due to lack of energy and time, we always resort to "shortcuts" in our everyday living but are they worth it? Instead of preparing home-cooked meals and making salads, we opt to grab on some burgers and instant foods full of artificial enhancers and preservatives. The meals are tasty and hassle-free but remember that it is your health that is at stake.

Maybe you are also too busy preparing a sales report and presentation for tomorrow that made you stay up late, or were you just being too obsessed with checking your social media accounts, and that's why you were sleepless? During weekends, do you allow at least a thirty-minute walk, or do you choose to collapse on your bed and gobble up some chips and ice cream?

A stressful way of living requires at least some healthy habits too. If you are guilty of these things, you should consider changing your unhealthy routines. To live a life of Zen involves healthy practices to attain a healthy state of mind. Being unhealthy has many side effects and risks; it makes you physically weak, emotionally unstable, and even affects your way of thinking.

9. Appreciate Mother Nature

In our life, we spend most of our time inside the office, our cars and vehicles, and inside our homes. We are so busy accomplishing our duties and responsibilities that we hardly get a chance to visit and spend time outside. During the weekends and holidays, when there is a chance to go on a vacation, most people choose to go to shopping malls instead of parks or gardens. There is no wrong in choosing where you want to spend your time, but you may want to consider spending time alone with Mother Nature.

There are numerous benefits of interacting with nature (psychologically, cognitively, socially, physiologically, and spiritually). Viewing the sceneries itself relaxes not only our eyes but also improves our moods. Scientifically, it is found that engaging in nature has a reflective impact on our intellects and behaviors. Nature is believed to help us reduce experiences of anxiety and stress. Thus, it helps develop creativity and improves our ability to connect with other people.

Try to go to a garden or a park. Sit down and observe how wonderful our nature is. Appreciate it and enjoy the moment. Breathe the fresh air coming from the trees, gaze on the greens, and relax your sight. Listen to the rustling of the leaves and the gentle breeze.

Nature can never be replaced by any type of hotel, mall, or other recreational area created artificially. Our nature is the only one that can provide us with breath-taking scenery, supply us fresh air, and improve our health issues.

Zen at Work

Regardless of what type of job we do, we must practice Zen every so often. Work, typically, is stressful. Whether it is related to your boss, your workmates, or the environment itself, everything related to work seems suffocating sometimes. Due to busy schedules and heavy workloads, we can't take vacations even if we need to. We make the most out of the time given to us in order to meet our deadlines and responsibilities. But how can we be committed to our jobs if we are constantly stressed and unmotivated?

1. **Slow things down**

    In a fast-paced world we are living in nowadays, it is ironic to think that even though technology helps us finish our jobs quicker and easier, we do not use that advantage efficiently. Instead of finding time to relax and enjoy after we have finished our work, we tend to waste our remaining energy abusing the internet, our gadgets, machines, etc.

    As the Buddha taught, to live a life of Zen is to acknowledge what is presently there. Technology, as we all know it, is manmade. Hence, we are all so caught up with it that we forget to enjoy the real things presently happening. Instead of clinging on to your phone, why not engage a conversation with a friend or a colleague? A cheerful greeting will cost you nothing; hence, it may even get you great connections. Learn to appreciate the stillness of the morning rather than rushing off to work just to be absorbed by technology again. These simple things teach us only one lesson—to slow down and delight in life even more.

When we are always in a hurry, we tend to oversight things. Hence, do tasks one at a time to improve your accuracy in doing your duties. Take time to finish one thing slowly but surely. Do not rush. The more you rush, the more you are prone to committing mistakes and missing details.

2. **Set aside work from your "me time"**
   Learn to manage your time wisely. Do not let your time for work and time for other things mix up. When you work, focus on your work alone to finish it on time, and

you won't have to sacrifice your "me time" for other responsibilities. Try to balance your time for work and play. You may want to create a schedule so you can track your time.

Most of the workforce encounters problems like this because they are not able to manage their time well.

3. Set daily reminders

Make a daily reminder of your meetings, appointments, and other errands so you can track your activities for the day. Include photos of your family or loved ones, your pet, your favorite quote, a beautiful destination, or even a background song that motivates you. In doing so, you can be more inspired to work, making you more productive. It also lessens the pressure and stress brought by work.

Daily reminders do not necessarily comprise activities and responsibilities. You can also use daily quotes and Bible verses that help you boost yourself and uplift you as a person. Sometimes, what others think about us is not what matters.

It is how we feel about ourselves that is more important at the end of the day.

4. **Do not work while eating**

Eating a nutritious lunch is a proven way to be healthy. It also boosts the immune system. Thus, when we are healthy, we tend to be more productive throughout the day. However, we must take note of where and with whom we eat our lunches. Certain researchers have said that improper lunch breaks have caused fatigue and unproductivity among employees and the workforce.

Hence, the best way to avoid this is to eat inside a cafeteria or a canteen instead of eating in front of your desk. Taking a proper break allows your brain to recharge and detach from the energy-draining issues at work.

Try not to answer calls and e-mails while you are eating. Stay away from things about work that could interfere with your lunchtime. Savor each bite of your food and resist the urge to talk about issues from work during lunch. Enjoy eating your meal, and use your time to rest or take a nap afterward. You may also take a walk or use that time for personal hygiene practices.

5. **Allocate a space or breathing area where you can calm down in times of stress and anxiety**

Take regular breaks and perform breathing exercises. This is a helpful Zen technique that you can apply during work. It can help you calm your senses and get you motivated again to go back to work.

You can also practice these techniques while you drink your tea or coffee. A minute of calmness is indeed helpful in stimulating one's mind.

6. **Create a healthy working environment**

Companies, offices, and workplaces are known to attract a lot of stress and pressure. A lot of times, we even get irritated or angered because of several factors. It may be due to an unfinished or wrong report that got you reprimanded by the boss, an annoying office mate, or you were just late due to traffic. Due to these reasons, we tend to exhibit bad behavior towards our peers.

By establishing a good relationship with your co-workers, you can create a happy and healthy working environment. Don't look at your superiors, colleagues, and subordinates as enemies or competitors. Instead, treat them as buddies. Appreciate your co-workers once in a while, not only when they have achievements and accomplishments but also with their good qualities.

Zen in Relationships

In Building relationships

Have you met someone, and for some reason, you've already judged him or her by the way he or she gives the impression to you? Most of the time, when we meet people and get interested in them, we are in a rush to know them. We think we've known them already, but really, we might be wrong.

The human mind is primarily empty in nature, meaning it is a state that requires judgment and knowledge in order to be full. An empty mind is always craving for something; hence, it is open for everything. But if we always rely on our judgment of people, we might miss prospect relationships. Deep connections are hard to find. The reason why this happens is because of our rash conclusions that lead to wrong impressions.

The role of Zen in relationships is to empty our minds so that we can be able to receive more wisdom and possibilities. Being able to do so, we understand how significant it is to learn more about a person by being more open and more curious about them.

- **Open yourself**
  The quality of open-mindedness to things is one of the key foundations of Zen Buddhism's beliefs and practices. It is an attribute that allows us to gain more knowledge of a certain person or event apart from the existing familiarity that we know from them. Thus, opening ourselves not only exposes us from a lot of opportunities but also makes us mentally stronger. When we are open to new experiences and ideas, we are honed to become more equipped and excited about the endless challenges that come along in

our lives. We become resilient and optimistic in everything, including our relationship issues.

Keeping an open mind is encouraging, but it can be a little bit challenging. The human mind is designed for viewing models of information as a whole. Thus, when our minds receive new information, we tend to undergo a mental process wherein our minds adjust to what we already know.

Misunderstandings and disagreements are a few of the main reasons why some relationships fail. Hence, in this chapter, I will share some proven ways that could guide us towards becoming an ideal open-minded person.

✓ Intellectual Humility

Being intellectually humble is a method of thinking in which a person does not resist any type of knowledge or information he or she is given, even though it is unfavorable in his or her part. Instead, he or she is more attentive to learn from others.

Researches have shown that sometimes, being well-informed about something can lead to closed-mindedness. This is for a fact that when we believe that we are knowledgeable of something, we tend to stop learning about it because we think that what we know is already enough.

Because of that, real experts tend to be essentially humble about their knowledge. They believe that learning never stops and that there is always something to learn from others. So, if you think that you already know everything, odds are you don't.

With this, we know that being closed-minded often leads to cognitive ignorance. It limits our wisdom of what others know and the opportunity to establish a relationship with them.

✓ **Take some time**
Before judging what you see or hear, take a little bit of time to

listen and consider what others have to say. Commonly among us humans, we tend to instantly disagree when someone talks about something. Instead of trying to listen, we easily heat up and prove how wrong the idea or the person is.

The problem with this kind of thinking is kin to our fast emotional response. Often, it is easier for us to criticize than to accept the diversity of things. As an alternative, giving ourselves an ample amount of time to mull over and evaluate thoughts before judgment can avoid arguments.

Being open-minded technically requires cognitive effort. If you aren't willing to consider other ideas and opinions, it may be really difficult to be open-minded. Dogmatism, in all its forms, contradicts the concept of what Zen Buddhism tries to demonstrate. Thus, to avoid this, taking a short time to evaluate your response first is recommended to avoid careless judgments and decisions.

Characteristics of an Open-minded person that can help build or save relationships

1. Believes that others have the right to share their beliefs and feelings
2. Welcomes other people's opinions and respects them
3. Does not get angry when wronged
4. Appreciates other people's suggestions and ideas
5. Loves new learnings and growth
6. Thinks positively even when things don't go as expected

In Saving Relationships

- Listen more, talk less
  When your partner or one person talks to you, do you listen to a reply or to understand? This is a good question to consider, especially when saving relationships. Most of the time, we are in

a rush to solve problems, which is why there is this natural tendency in us to only just communicate and not comprehend. When we merely communicate, we are only talking without addressing the topic or the problem. But when we comprehend, we are giving our full attention to the person and the topic.

The good thing about this concept is its applicability to every type of relationship—from a beginning friendship or a long-term relationship. Misunderstandings happen at times. Whether we are creating friendships or saving relationships, the best thing that we can give to a person is respect and understanding. When we are able to make someone feel understood, we are giving them an extraordinary gift that not everyone can give. With this, a sense of trust is being established in both parties.

Becoming Stronger in Relationships

- Let go
  Break up, death of a loved one, feud with a colleague, misunderstandings,

traumatic experiences—these are some of the many reasons why a person can feel frustrated and lost in life.

Such events are expected to be experienced in this world. It is part of human nature to get caught up with such episodes at a certain point in our lives. Consequently, the Buddha's teachings encourage us to persevere amid difficulties.

The path to enlightenment aims to free us from any form of hatred and resentment towards a person or an experience in the past. By letting go, we can understand ourselves more deeply, become stronger, and be exposed to all kinds of predicaments that we may encounter in the future.

Letting go means you are willing to let go of anything, big or small, that holds you back into living your life peacefully and freely. If you have any emotional baggage from past experiences, you may start by listing them in a journal. Each day, write about what you feel. Have you been okay lately? What are the things you are currently up to? Are there things bothering you? Ask yourself these questions and evaluate your present situation.

Take time to heal yourself from past trauma and help yourself recover. Sometimes, all it takes to move on is to just accept what has gone, let it go, and find something to look forward to.

Key Points

- Zen Buddhism is more than just practicing Zen meditation. It can be applied to various aspects of life.
- Zen Buddhism can help you learn how to let go and achieve freedom. It can help you heal and move on.
- You must learn to let go, no matter how big or small it is.
- Zen Buddhism teaches you to adopt the right traits and/or characteristics that are necessary for achieving true happiness and peace.
- A life of Zen is a life that revolves around the present moment. It does not hold on to the past or get anxious about the future.

CHAPTER SIX

Transforming Your State of Mind through Kindness and Compassion

"When there are thoughts,

It is distraction:

When there are no thoughts,

It is meditation."

-Ramana Maharshi

Life, as you know it, is difficult. This is why compassion is necessary. Everyone is prone to injuries and diseases. Everyone has a life that inevitably starts and ends. Everyone encounters unexpected events and experiences. No one can ever escape the uncertainties of life.

It would be much easier to go through life with compassion. When people work together, journeys become more bearable. There is a Buddhist tradition that describes this. It says that just like others, you wish to be happy. Likewise, just like everyone else, you wish to be free of suffering.

Such recognition of common yearning and fear is where compassion stems from. Although compassion may not be very easy, its general view is simple. Compassionate individuals are sensitive to suffering as well as committed to trying to prevent and alleviate it.

Take note that suffering must not be confused with any positive emotions, such as love, because the most difficult form of compassion is for those who you love. Likewise, it is much more difficult to have compassion towards people who are not like you. You have probably felt more compassionate towards those who share similar interests or points of view with you.

In addition, your experiences in life may also diminish your ability to receive and give compassion. More often than not, those who attend therapy get entangled in psychological loops that hinder their ability to receive compassion from themselves or other people.

Nevertheless, it is possible to break such loops when you become aware of the way your brain works. In other words, you can break from your psychological loop if you can be aware of your own awareness.

Once you are able to do that, you can start to cultivate compassion. You can learn how to cultivate compassionate thinking, compassionate attention, compassionate behavior, and compassionate feeling. You can also learn how to be open towards the suffering of other people, aside from the suffering in yourself. This would help you act towards alleviating such suffering.

The Relation between Suffering and Your Brain

According to biology, your brain is created by your genes. Hence, you did not have any control over its development. It was controlled by evolution. While it is true that your brain can do so many great things, such as finding ways to treat and cure diseases, it can also do a lot of awful things, such as starting a war.

The way your brain has evolved means that it can give you trouble. In fact, you have two brains—an old one and a new one.

Your old brain has desires and motives that have already evolved years ago. You share this experience with other animals. Just take a look around you and observe your surroundings. For instance, you may notice that your pet dog avoids things that may harm it. It may bark at anything that looks unusual. It may also be territorial and possessive. Moreover, dogs are naturally concerned with hierarchy. This is why there is such a thing as an alpha dog.

Humans are just the same. They are also concerned about their status, particularly in society. They like to be part of groups as well as are inclined to develop friendships and personal connections. They are also naturally inclined to reproduce and take care of their offspring. Furthermore, humans do their best to avoid anything that might bring them harm. They also feel happiness, sadness, anger, and a wide variety of emotions.

Then again, humans are a lot different from other animals. Millions of years ago, ancient humans began to evolve and developed intelligence. This explains why you are capable of reasoning, visualizing, using symbols, and using language.

This new brain of yours is amazing when you use it wisely. Then again, you have to keep in mind that this also depends on the way you use it with your old brain.

Say, you spot a lion and a zebra in the same area. Once the zebra sees the lion, it would surely run away. This is its natural instinct. It knows that its life would be in danger if it does not stay away from the lion.

Your old brain works the same way. It has a primal instinct to detect and respond to threats. So, when the zebra successfully escapes, it would head back to its herd to eat and live. It would not recall the recent event.

Then again, there is a new brain. It is what makes humans different from wild animals. Since you are a human being, you would think about the possible consequences of your actions. You would ponder on what just happened. You would also probably wonder what you could have done differently if you were in the position of the zebra.

This is also the reason why you think about the future. Your new brain allows you to plan ahead of time so that you can increase your odds of getting what you want. You can also think of the steps that you may have to take in order to stay safe and secure.

Even though this is helpful and beneficial, it is also quite disadvantageous. Anxiety, for instance, is a usual result of thinking using your new brain. The threat may have long been gone, but your new brain still holds onto it. It simply cannot let go that easily.

Human beings tend to run simulations in their heads. They tend to ruminate and visualize "what if" scenarios. If they are not able to control their thinking, they can become anxious and depressed. They can also be in constant fear of the future.

The Emotional Memory

Humans also have an emotional memory. For example, you love holidays. Whenever there is a holiday coming up, you become excited. You look forward to the festivities and seeing your family or friends. You start to pick out clothes or even shop for new ones. You are always in a good mood when there is an upcoming holiday.

But what happens if you experience something bad during your favorite time of the year? Say, you get beaten up by a random group of men. They robbed you, and you eventually end up in a hospital. Your holiday is ruined. You no longer associate your favorite time of the year with fun and festivities. Because of this unfortunate event, you no longer become excited. Even worse, the incident has left you traumatized. You become anxious every time you remember it, especially around the holidays.

This very same mechanism works with children who experience trauma in the hands of their parents or caregivers. Humans have an attachment system in which part of their brain facilitates the loving connection with their parents. Then again, this part also gets connected to the fear system. Hence, if a child grows up in a toxic environment, he tends to form unhealthy attachments with other people in adulthood. His emotional memory becomes unpleasant, and he becomes prone to mental health disorders.

A lot of people have mental health issues. They become stuck in a loop, ruminating about the things that make them fearful and anxious. They solely focus on the negative; they reject the positive.

It is important to take note that this is not their fault. They simply have an old brain threat bias. According to Dr. Rick Hanson, a psychologist and author, the brain works like a Velcro for threat-biased and negative things. Conversely, it works like a Teflon for positive things.

Mindfulness as the Solution

Humans indeed have an old brain and new brain that makes them happy and sad and courageous and fearful at the same time. If you ever feel anxious at times, you should not worry too much about it. Know that you are also capable of reconciling your new brain with your old brain.

You can use the mindfulness technique. It involves moment-to-moment awareness of feelings and thoughts. Every human being is capable of being aware of awareness. Thus, you are capable of observing and learning about the tricks that your mind plays on you.

Mindfulness is such a vital and wondrous evolutionary quality. In fact, it is akin to the development of a visual system. Take light, for instance. It exists. However, it cannot be perceived by anyone or anything that is not capable of being aware of it.

Since you are a human being, you are capable of being aware of light as well as life. Unlike wild animals, you do not simply go throughout your day eating and sleeping. You also spend time thinking of what you want to do, such as losing weight and becoming fitter.

With mindfulness, you can understand that attention is similar to the spotlight in the sense that whatever it focuses upon becomes brighter and emphasized. So, in your mind, whatever thought you focus upon would become more profound and affect you more significantly.

To help you understand this further, you can try visualizing yourself going on a vacation. Imagine that you have finally gone on the trip of your dreams. You are feeling very excited. You have finally experienced going to your dream destination and doing what you have always wanted to do all your life.

Focus on this thought for one minute. Observe your body. What happens when you dedicate an entire minute to this thought alone? Do you feel any sensations? What are these sensations?

When the minute has passed, you can purposely think of something else. Switch your focus and attention to another thought, particularly one that worries or concerns you. Focus on this thought for one minute, and just like what you did before, observe its effects on your body. Does the concerning or disturbing thought make you feel differently? How does it make you feel?

While attention or focus can bring things into the spotlight, it can also take it out of it. It can bring things into the dark. For example, you are doing your Christmas shopping. You go inside ten shops with nine of them having very helpful sales personnel. In one of the shops, you encounter a rude salesperson. This person makes you wait and does not answer your questions about the products being sold in the store.

Because of this experience, you are able to remember this one rude person out of all the others. This particular salesperson stands out from the rest of the sales personnel you have encountered throughout the day. Even if you go to more shops, you will still remember this person if the sales personnel in the other shops are also friendly and helpful.

When you reach home, you may still think about your recent experience. You may ruminate and think about possible consequences. You may have "what ifs" as well as wonder why some people act that way. You may wonder whether you should report the incident to the store manager or just let it go. You may also wish for the rude salesperson to lose his job.

This puts you in a loop. You stay in an anger system for a significant period of time. You do not think of the other sales personnel who were friendly and helpful. You merely focus on the one who was rude and unhelpful to you. The helpful ones stay in the dark while the unhelpful one stays in the spotlight. This example shows how people forget a huge part of their experience by focusing on just one thing, particularly a negative one.

Then again, the moment you notice what your mind is up to as well as determine why it is up to it, you can take control over your attention. You are also able to use it practically and mindfully.

So, going back to the previous example, you can purposely bring your thought back to the other nine helpful sales personnel. You can exert effort to remember how friendly and nice they were to you. You can recall how you were able to find what you want and felt happy about it. Such thought can put you in a good mood and allow you to forget about your unpleasant experience with the rude salesperson.

When you take this step, you can break out of your anger loop. Nonetheless, this step requires your attention, which is the key to developing compassion.

Keep in mind that compassion stems from your brain system. It has a lot to do with motivation and intentionality. When you orient yourself towards compassion, you can change the entire orientation of your mind.

The key is to understand and know that you have the capacity to purposely select your basic motivational system. For instance, you can consciously choose a motivational system for caring and then cultivate it. You can also make it grow through consistent practice.

In addition, you have to know exactly why it is important to do this. Well, you need to do this because it changes your brain and gives you more control of your life.

Courage and Compassion

With therapy, you can develop compassion. You can be trained to recall and observe kindness as well as build upon your memories. Matthieu Ricard, author and Buddhist monk, says that the mind is like a garden that grows naturally. If it is left uncultivated, it can be influenced by external elements such as the wind. It can also be affected by the changing weather. Some things tend to grow large, while others tend to shrivel. In the end, some of the results may not be favorable to you.

As a human being, you have the capability to understand how and why you need to cultivate compassion within yourself. This, in turn, would let you heal and reorganize your mind so that you can become the person that you want to be.

However, you also need to be courageous. For instance, if you are agoraphobic, you have to do some modifications to your behavior. You will not achieve compassion by always staying at home, wallowing, and doing easy things. You need to have the courage to face your fears as well as overcome your anxieties.

In essence, there are two kinds of courage: physical and emotional. Many men possess physical courage, but only a few possess emotional courage, which involves the ability to navigate into areas of deep pain and suffering.

When you have compassion, you would be able to move in these areas. However, you also need to be prepared to confront and alleviating the pain within yourself.

Your old brain and new brain can both be a blessing and a curse. It all depends on how you use them. Your old brain, in particular, should be used wisely. You must not allow yourself to get lost in your basic motives and emotions. You must also refrain from being distressed and too affected by the issues of other people.

Thanks to evolution, you have been given an extraordinary competency that allows you to sense and experience the consciousness of consciousness. The nature of your mind is so wonderful that you can cultivate the necessary emotions in your life. You can be awakened and enlightened.

Key Takeaways

- Humans are evolved creatures that possess both an old brain and a new brain. Your old brain makes you akin to wild animals while your new brain differentiates you from them.

- The old brain and the new brain can both be a blessing and a curse depending on how they are used.

- It is necessary to learn how to use your new brain properly in order for you to reap its benefits and/or rewards. If you are not able to use it wisely, then it will not work in your favor.

- Kindness and compassion can transform your state of mind and allow you to be free from worries and stress.

- Humans are wonderful creatures with lots of possibilities. They can cultivate compassion as well as understand why it has to be cultivated within oneself.

- Compassion may not be very easy to develop. Nevertheless, it can be done with the help of therapy.

- Mindfulness can solve problems that relate to stress and anxiety brought about by human feelings and thoughts.

CHAPTER SEVEN

Center Your Life and Awaken Inner Peace with Zen Buddhism

"Meditation makes the entire nervous system

Go into a field of coherence."

-Deepak Chopra

The Zen practice is the way to true happiness and peace. Zen Buddhism shows you the way. The Buddha taught people how to achieve enlightenment. However, he did not elaborate on what it was.

It is important to note that concepts may have a certain importance. Then again, it is the actual path that is much more important. Simply thinking of what something may be like without actually knowing it or walking the path on your own does not really matter.

Zen Buddhism is about direct experience. When you study the schools of Buddhism, make sure that you study the "sutras" or the texts as well as practice using your direct experience.

Remember that the Buddha told his disciples to never follow or believe in anything that they merely heard. They should not readily follow anyone, including himself, without proper judgment.

This part of Buddhism is appreciated by many, including myself. Doing something based on blind faith alone is indeed ridiculous. One must always study the text and use wisdom to verify its authenticity. Each and every one of us is gifted with a wonderful mind. Therefore, we should use it.

The practice of Buddhism can be ultimately described as the process of working to gain moments of insight, including the ones gained from direct experience.

What Zen Is All About

True change can only happen when we experience things for ourselves. This might seem a little overwhelming, but it is necessary. Hence, you must not hesitate to ask yourself questions that would eventually lead you to the right answers.

Keep in mind that Zen is about slowing down. More often than not, people live in such a hurry that they no longer become mindful of what they are doing. They tend to go on autopilot and do everything on a routine.

While it can be practical to go on your daily routine, it can also hinder your spiritual growth. Speeding things up to save you time robs you of the opportunity to reflect, meditate, and practice mindfulness. You need to learn how to slow down when necessary. Do not worry because you will still be productive.

Other things that people want are fame, power, and money. Sadly, many of them believe that these things will bring them genuine happiness. With Zen, you will learn that this kind of thinking is wrong and dangerous. If all you do is chase after success and material wealth, you will not be content. You will not feel any satisfaction, no matter how rich and powerful you become. You will not be happy.

Zen is about being peaceful, content, and happy. Zen is also about having understanding and compassion. You must not harbor ill feelings towards others. You must learn to forgive and let go. It is only when you can do this that you would truly heal and be at peace. Furthermore, you must remember that everyone is connected intrinsically. So, whatever you do onto other people, you also do to yourself.

Through Zen, you can achieve genuine happiness and peace. It can teach you how to work from within yourself, see through illusions, discover your real nature, and break free from attachments.

Let's say you have your own business. Your business should treat everyone with compassion. Teach your employees to nurture and support the well-being of one another. Likewise, they should learn how to treat customers and/or clients fairly.

When you do not solely focus on making money, you can treat other people and yourself with compassion. This would allow you to achieve genuine happiness and peace.

How Practicing Zen Changes Lives

The practice of Zen is recommended to everyone, regardless of age, gender, or social status.

Zazen or Sitting Meditation

Zazen, also referred to as sitting meditation, creates a significant impact on the lives of people. I, myself, for example, have never been prone to anxiety and stress. However, when my first child was born, I have begun to feel as if time constantly runs out. I recalled my past actions and thought that I had not had any major life achievements. As a result, I forced myself to do something great; but this only made me more prone to anxiety and stress.

One day, I learned about Zen Buddhism, and I was fascinated. So, I started meditating right away. Several weeks later, I noticed that my anxiety and stress had been significantly reduced. It was as if I was a completely new person! I realized that practicing meditation has made me more productive and less stressed. My chaotic mind has finally attained peace.

Through Zen Buddhism, I became a much happier person. I now find contentment in everything. I feel happiness in everything I do. I also feel more resilient. Each time a challenge comes my way, I can face it without worries or doubts. I know that I can do it. I know in my heart that whatever outcome I get, I can surely accept it.

For this, I highly recommend zazen or sitting meditation. If you are a beginner, you can find tips and information online. There are plenty of websites and articles that you can check out. You can also watch tutorial videos or read books about this topic. Once you have been introduced to this practice, you can start living a new life using Zen Buddhism.

Mindfulness Meditation

Frequently, people become so immersed in their jobs and daily chores. Rather than become mindful of what they are doing, they move on autopilot. This causes them to miss out on the beauty and wonders of life. They become so focused on their work that they no longer have time to relax and refresh their minds.

Through mindfulness meditation, you can reprogram your life. Mindfulness is actually meditation in action. According to Thich Nhat Hanh, Zen master, mindfulness is about keeping your consciousness alive to the current reality. In essence, it means following your breath.

Every living creature breathes. So, no matter what you do, you breathe. This is why breathing is such a good anchor. When you keep your focus on your breathing, you remain grounded in your present moment. Whether you walk, talk, or do something else, you can focus on your breath. When you do this, you practice mindfulness.

You see, there are lots of advantages to mindfulness. So, you should always take a moment to notice and follow your breath. You can also practice mindfulness as you walk, sit, or lay down. This can help you regain a sense of happiness and peace and allow you to regain control of your emotions.

Like I mentioned previously, I used to have a chaotic mind. It was only when I learned about practicing meditation that I was able to gain peace. I used to be anxious and worried about not having enough time for my tasks. I was always in a hurry.

Now that I have learned to practice meditation, I no longer feel the anxiousness or the need to rush everything. I feel that I have ample time to do everything I have to do. No matter what I do, I feel that the moment is mine. This allows me to be more peaceful yet productive.

You, too, can be peaceful and productive at the same time. Mindfulness would nourish your mind and body. It would enable you to find genuine happiness and peace instead of the shallow and temporary fixes of material things and nonsensical activities.

Compassion Cultivation

Through Buddhism, you can learn about developing compassion. Compassion is a major aspect of every Buddhism teaching, including Zen. According to the Dalai Lama, compassion is not merely a passion emotion but rather an aspiration. Thus, one must work on expressing it towards other people. When you can do this, you can realize the real nature of your existence as well as discover a deeper sense of happiness and peace.

The teachings of the Buddha also emphasize enlightenment. For you to achieve enlightenment, you need to have compassion and wisdom. Some people find this difficult, but it can be done in simple ways.

For example, you can start by being kinder to other people. As you continue to do this, you would eventually realize that it is fulfilling to do something good for other people without expecting anything in return. If you still harbor the thinking of needing to get something in return, then you are not yet truly wise and enlightened.

The illusion of self is, in fact, the greatest illusion. Through compassion, you would see this truth. Once you become enlightened, you would awaken from such illusion. You would learn how to eradicate attachments and illusions as well as look deeper within yourself.

Discovery of the Real Path to Happiness

A lot of people think that the real path to happiness involves money, success, and power. However, this is not true. Material wealth, for instance, only brings shallow and temporary happiness. Even those who believe that chasing their dreams would make them happy are wrong. The truth is that genuine happiness exists within yourself, not outside.

When you can use mindfulness and live fully in the present moment, you can achieve happiness and peace. Use sitting meditation to look deeply within yourself and treat everybody with compassion. Do not worry because this kind of happiness is unlimited. You can renew it as much as possible, as long as you take control of your happiness.

Learning About Mindful Consumption

Everything you use and consume creates a significant impact on your life. So, everything that you eat, watch, listen to, and take makes you the person that you are.

If you are like most people, you probably complain a lot about your job, your boss, your co-workers, your relationship, etc. You also probably talk about others behind their backs or engage in gossip and drama. All of these actions have a negative impact on yourself.

Fortunately, you can still bounce back and have a mindful consumption. Take one step at a time. For example, you can begin with quitting television and reading a book instead. Whenever you have free time, you can pick up a self-help book to improve your wellbeing. Ditch the habit of watching television, for it does nothing helpful to you.

You can also learn a new skill by watching tutorials. Likewise, you can expand your knowledge by reading articles or listening to podcasts. Do your best to more productive during your free time.

Next, you should work on your communication skills. Improve your conversations with people at home, at work, and in the community. You can enroll in language courses and take classes, whether offline or online. You can practice what you have learned by being more outspoken, engaging in small talk, and joining clubs. Make your social circle bigger so that you can communicate with more people.

These simple activities are effective in helping individuals make changes that have profound results. Keep in mind that it is easy to change the things that you consume as well as change the ways you act and feel. What's more, it is alright to be imperfect. You may devise plans and end up not following them exactly. That is alright, as long as you stay focused and continue to create progress.

Discovery of Your True Nature

If you aim to find the purpose of your life, you cannot use Zen to do that. However, you can use Zen to discover your true nature.

A lot of people are searching for their life purpose, and many of them are searching in the wrong places. Through Zen Buddhism, you can fulfill your desire to feel found and connected. This is even though you do not find your purpose.

You will learn that the part of your nature that you see is not really you. The "small you," which you see is not your true nature, but rather the "big you" that you have to discover.

Thich Nhat Hanh explains that the "small you" is merely the phenomenal world or the world you see and know. It is merely a wave. The "big you," on the other hand, is the noumenal world or the ultimate dimension wherein there is no separation between you and others.

Take note that Zen Buddhism is not about understanding, but rather about gaining insight and direct experience. In order for you to start heading to the path of gaining insights and learning about your true nature, you need to practice. This means that you have to practice Zen meditation.

The takeaway is for you to know that what you want is not a sense of purpose but rather a sense of connection. You want to connect to the whole world around you.

In general, this sense of connection with others can cause you to want to contribute to the greater good. When you contribute, you will be able to find a deep sense of connection with others.

There are so many things you can do throughout your lifetime. Nonetheless, whatever you opt to focus on, see to it that it lets you help other people. This would make you feel the sense of fulfillment and sense of connection you have been searching for.

Simplification of Life

Through Zen Buddhism, you can learn how to make your life simpler yet more fulfilling. If you practice mindfulness and Zen meditation, the mental and physical illusions that have been right in front of you would be naturally revealed. This, in turn, would free you from any desires for material things that you may have.

Now, you have to take note that there is nothing wrong with wanting more for your life. You can desire a better job, a bigger house, a newer car, or more money, especially if your reasons are justifiable, such as wanting a much better life for your family. Then again, even though this is the case, you still have to remember that true happiness and peace will not stem from material things.

The Buddhist practice states that one must be aware of the illusions that are present around him. He must see reality as it is. Likewise, he must see the illusion as it is. This is primarily referred to as mental illusions in Buddhism.

There isn't a separation. The physical things in your life exist because you found them necessary to be there. The moment you realize that an idea is merely an illusion, you will be able to set yourself free from it.

Seeing clarity is a good natural byproduct of Zen Buddhism, and it is something that everyone can benefit from, especially today. Then again, you must keep in mind that it is only possible to properly understand Zen through direct experiences.

You can read all the books you want, watch every video online, or take tons of classes, but it is only when you have had a direct experience that you would truly understand Zen.

Key Points

- If you want to make significant changes in your life, you must learn to practice Zen Buddhism.
- Clarity is a natural byproduct of Zen Buddhism that many people can benefit from.
- It is only through direct experiences that you can truly understand Zen.
- Zen Buddhism focuses on gaining insights and direct experiences, not merely trying to understand its concept.
- As a human being, you have both a "small self" and a "big self" that you need to fully understand in order to get to know yourself.
- The actual path of Zen Buddhism is much more important than its concept.

CHAPTER EIGHT

Zen Is for Everybody

It Can Be Practiced by Both Beginners and Individuals Who Are Either Continuing With or Returning to Buddhism

"Zen is not some kind of excitement,

But concentration on our usual everyday routine."

-Shunryu Suzuki

Buddhism is a spiritual tradition that mainly focuses on spiritual growth and development. It also focuses on the attainment of a deeper insight into the real nature of life. According to Buddhist teachings, life is endless and filled with suffering, uncertainty, and impermanence.

Buddhism is regarded as an ancient Eastern religion by many people, specifically those who turn to it to help them deal with various mental health issues.

Now, even though a lot of people have already turned to Buddhism, there are still some who are still confused and skeptical about it. They want to find out why it is preferred by many and whether or not it is worth practicing.

Before we discuss this topic further, let us first have an overview of why Buddhism is ideal for beginners, including Westerners, and why many people are into it.

Why Do People Like Buddhism?

First of all, it is important to note that Buddhists are generally not aggressive at seeking out converts. Unlike other religious groups, they do not give out brochures or stand on the streets to prompt strangers to adopt their beliefs. They usually go about on their own until others seek their help for conversion or assistance.

Buddhism is also not dogmatic. This means that it does not believe in demons or devils. Buddhists do not believe in dogma, so they have the freedom to study and examine the doctrine of Buddhism. They are not prevented by lies and fears to think outside of their beliefs.

Likewise, Buddhists do not believe in a god or deity the way Christians do. They do not believe that there is a "God" who sits on a throne in heaven and watches everything that man does. Instead, they believe that nothing is permanent or fixed in the world, and that change is always a possibility.

With this being said, Buddhists do not live in fear of suffering for eternity if they do something that does not please "God." The belief that there is permanence is a cause for suffering.

According to Buddhist teachings, there is no state of good or bad that lasts forever. Everything is impermanent, and that the path towards enlightenment is through the development and practice of morality, wisdom, and meditation.

These are the primary reasons why more and more people are turning to Buddhism. Even those who have left to explore other religious practices have come back due to the numerous benefits the Buddhist philosophy gives them.

In addition, a lot of people do not like the conservativeness of certain religions, such as Judaism and Christianity. They also do not appreciate being told to do a certain thing or have a particular belief to be "saved." They prefer to live with an open mind and a conscience, but without the dogma.

Buddhism helps people achieve enlightenment and inner calm. It encourages them to look inwards as well as develop compassion, which is the way to overcoming fear and suffering. So, when you practice Buddhism, you would need to master yourself rather than solely believe and rely on a god.

Why Do People Turn to Spirituality and Religion?

There are various reasons why people turn to spirituality and religion. For instance, anxiety, deprivation, fear, and frustration can be factors in driving a person towards prayer and faith.

When people experience grief, hopelessness, or fear, they may look for an outlet or external source that they believe might save or help them. Both positive and negative experiences and emotions can drive people towards spirituality and religion.

This is why most people pray when they feel hopeless and desperate. They pray that their loved one be healed from a sickness, their relationship is fixed, or their financial status gets better. It is not surprising to find churches filled with devotees who pray to their chosen deity or saint for divine assistance.

Conversely, people also pray when they are overjoyed and grateful. They pray to give thanks for the blessings they have, such as getting a new job or winning a competition. Published studies by Saroglou, Buxant, and Tilquin have explored the causal relationship between spirituality and religion and positive emotions.

Also, self-growth motives can lead people towards spirituality and religion. Aside from the compensation needs in the cognitive and affective sphere, spirituality and religion can also be characterized by the motivations that denote self-development and self-realization.

Furthermore, spirituality and religion can play a crucial role in mental health. Sadly, many people who suffer from mental disorders do not have enough money for therapy. This is why they enroll in meditation classes, which are far less expensive. These classes help alleviate the stress and anxiety that they feel.

According to a Pew Research Center study done in 2012, about eighty percent of Americans claim that they practice spirituality and religiosity.

About twenty percent, on the other hand, claim that they do not believe in religion.

It was found that many people generally turn to faith as a form of support and solace, especially during stressful situations. Certain groups, including minorities and seniors, also tend to turn to faith rather than family and friends.

Those who deal with major stressors in life, such as loss of a loved one, divorce, serious mental and physical illnesses, and natural diseases, tend to find spirituality and religion helpful in their coping. This is especially true for those who have limited resources in dealing with uncontrollable situations.

Key Points

- Buddhism is a spiritual tradition that focuses on spiritual growth and development.
- Buddhism is not dogmatic. Buddhists do not believe in deities.
- Buddhist teachings state that no state of good or bad lasts forever because nothing is permanent.

- People turn to spirituality and religion for a variety of purposes.

CHAPTER NINE

Center Your Life and Attain Inner Peace with Zen Buddhism

"Before enlightenment, chop wood and carry water.

After enlightenment, chop wood and carry water."

-Wu Li

For those who are not that familiar with Buddhism, the first noble truth may seem quite gloomy. Buddhists believe that life is filled with misery, pain, and suffering. You go through life experiencing stress, anxiety, natural disasters, family problems, broken relationships, physical and mental illnesses, and financial losses, among others. Then, you die.

Yes, you may experience happiness at certain points in your life. However, you still cannot deny the fact that there is suffering. Suffering is inevitable. Nobody can escape from it.

The Buddha believed that one's attitude towards life events is far more important than broken legs or thunderstorms. By nature, humans tend to consistently desire things that they do not have. Conversely, they tend to dislike the things that they do have. Such an attitude causes them to experience mental anguish.

According to Buddha, sufferings are mainly experienced due to the endless sense of lacking permanent and basic security. Life's happenstance just cannot provide it.

In addition, the Buddha claimed that there is a way beyond suffering, and it involves replacing ignorance with the wisdom of knowing. When you can possess this kind of wisdom, you will be able to forego suffering.

Essentially, you must practice being "right," which means being mindful. You need to be mindful of your speech and actions, for example, to live a good life or a life with the Zen spirit.

I believe that everyone holds a pearl of intuitive wisdom within themselves, and it is this wisdom that hits their interconnected and harmonious nature. Likewise, it is this wisdom that brings the world together in harmony and peace. This wisdom is the very spirit of Zen.

Zen Meditation and the Real Key to Happiness

Zen mainly emphasizes the practice of meditation. It emits an essence that directly speaks to those who practice it. Zen can be an antidote to a variety of problems in the modern world. You can read about this in the Introduction of the book Zen Keys by Thich Nhat Hanh. The Introduction was written by Philip Kapleau, an author and teacher of Zen.

Contrary to what most people believe, the real key to happiness is neither wealth nor fame. The real key to happiness cannot be found externally because it lies within yourself. Buddhism teaches people that the more you give, the more you gain. You must also be aware of interconnectedness as well as appreciate every little gift that life offers you.

The more your compassion and concern for other people grow, the more personal fulfillment you will achieve. Keep in mind that if you search for inner peace, you will not find it. You must learn how to give up the idea of this reward and focus on the happiness of other people to create lasting peace. This is the true Zen spiritual dimension.

Zen helps the mind achieve calmness. When you meditate, you allow yourself to reflect with improved creativity and focus. You are also able to improve your health. Some of the benefits you can get include lower levels of anxiety, stress, and blood pressure. You can also have a stronger immune system as well as sleep better.

So, what are the Zen meditation techniques that you have to learn? Well, you should take note of the following:

Breath Observation

When you meditate, you must be in a comfortable position. For example, you can choose from the Burmese, Seiza, or Half-Lotus poses during zazen. Ideally, you should sit on a cushion or padded mat. However, if you do not have any of these items or cannot sit on the ground, you may also sit on a chair.

You must direct your awareness towards a particular object and focus on your breathing. Notice the way your breath moves in and out of your system. Doing this would foster a sense of alertness and peace.

Quiet Awareness

When you practice quiet awareness, you do not repose on any focal point, such as your breath. Instead, you allow your thoughts to move through your mind without rejection, judgment, or grasping. This practice is known as "just sitting" or *Shikantaza* in Japanese. It is practiced without any object of meditation, content, or anchor.

There is no need for you to aim for anything when you practice this meditation technique. You just have to sit and allow your mind to move freely. Remember that zazen is the end and not a means towards it.

Intensive Group Meditation

If you are truly serious about meditating, you can go to a temple or meditation center. This practice is referred to as Sesshin by the Japanese. During this time, you practice intensive meditation through sitting meditation.

A session can last between thirty and fifty minutes. You can switch to walking meditation from time to time or take a short break. When it is time to eat your meal, you must be silent. You must also use an oryoki bowl if possible. Likewise, when it is time to do work, you must be mindful.

Of course, when you practice Zen meditation, see to it that you practice it with mindfulness energy. You must be completely aware of every moment. Meditate with single-pointed awareness.

For example, when you clean, you must be completely present for this act. When you are with your loved ones, you must be completely present for them. When you relax at home, you must be completely present for it. Do not allow anything to distract you. Refrain from occupying your mind with anxieties and worries.

You should also meditate naturally and simply. Understand that less is more. When you can accept this, your state of mind will improve. You must learn how to accept things as they come and go.

What's more, you have to be loving and compassionate. Be concerned not only for your well-being but for the well-being of other people as well. Keep in mind that everything and everyone in this world is interconnected.

Develop the habit of doing one thing at a time. Zen monks believe that it is much better to single-task than to multi-task. For example, when you have to pour water in your cup, you should pour water in your cup without doing anything else, such as listening to the morning news. Likewise, when you eat, you must focus on eating. Do not eat while watching TV or reading the newspaper.

Zen monks also do things deliberately and slowly. They do not rush their activities. You, too, should develop this habit. Rather than act randomly and rushed, you have to act in a deliberate matter.

Focus on a particular task. Refrain from moving on to another task without completing the current one. Then again, if there comes a time when you do not have any other option but to do something else, you should at least try to set aside your unfinished task and then clean up.

For example, when you make a sandwich, you should not begin eating until you have put away the bowls, spoons, bread knife, and ingredients that you have used. You should not begin enjoying your meal until you are done wiping your counter and washing the dishes. Once you are done cleaning up, then you can go ahead and enjoy your sandwich. Your first task, essentially, is cleaning up while your second task is eating.

As mentioned previously, doing less is doing more. Zen monks are not lazy, but they do believe in doing less and not rushing things. They wake up early in the morning and start doing their chores. Their days are filled with tasks, but they do not try to accomplish everything in a day if it means having to rush them. They do their chores slowly, deliberately, and completely. They focus intently on every task they do. Once they are truly done with a certain task, then that is the only time they move on to the next one.

You should also learn how to put a space between tasks. This is similar to doing more with less. It is a way on how to effectively manage your schedule so that you can have ample time to complete your tasks. As much as possible, you have to refrain from scheduling everything so close to one another. You must always leave room between them to take a short break and refresh your mind. Having a more relaxed schedule allows you to focus better on every task.

Do not forget to have your ritual. Zen monks, as you know, have rituals that guide them in everything they do, from meditating to eating to sleeping. Rituals give things a sense of importance. So, if a task is important enough for you to give it a ritual, then it is important enough to be completely focused upon. There is no need for you to follow the exact rituals of Zen monks. You can develop your own. Just make sure that you stick to it.

Of course, you also have to make time for everything that needs to be done. You need to allot a particular schedule for a particular task or activity. For example, you need to designate a specific hour for taking a shower, preparing a meal, eating, commuting to work, doing work, and meditating.

This practice helps you develop a habit so that you can do such activities regularly. When you have a habit, your mind and body automatically get into doing the task. Do not forget about it. Thus, you can successfully do it.

Devote some time to siting. Zen monks practice zazen or sitting meditation daily. They allocate a specific hour for this activity. Sitting meditation allows them to focus on the present moment. You, too, should practice sitting meditation to clear your mind and relax your body.

Besides practicing sitting meditation, cooking and cleaning are also regular parts of a Zen monk's day. These chores also allow them to practice mindfulness. You can have this ritual too. You can treat cooking and cleaning as forms of mindfulness meditation. Completely focus on these tasks as you do them slowly.

Furthermore, you have to live simply. Only use what is necessary. For example, rather than have a closet filled with shoes, you can give away the pairs that you do not use anymore and just keep the ones that you use. Likewise, you should get rid of the clothes that only serve as clutter in your closet. Refrain from buying new things, especially if you merely want to follow the latest trend in fashion.

Zen monks live simply. They only think of what is necessary. They do not buy trendy clothes, shoes, and bags. They are not fond of the latest gadgets. They do not even eat fancy foods. Most of the time, their diet consists of rice, soup, and vegetables. They only have the basics, but they are happy and content. This is what living a life of Zen is all about. You can be simply but still happy.

Key Points

- The noble truths of Buddhism are well understood by those who truly know Buddhism.

- Buddhists believe that attitude towards life is the most important of all.

- Practicing Zen meditation can lead you to the path of true happiness.

- There are various Zen meditation techniques that you have to learn in order for you to be able to practice Zen meditation properly.

- Following in the footsteps of Zen monks and living like the way they do can help you achieve true happiness and inner peace.

CHAPTER TEN

A Beginner's Guide to Daily Zen Mindfulness

"Mindfulness isn't difficult,

We just need to remember to do it."

-Sharon Salzberg

Developing the habit of meditation is among the best things you can do. Meditating is simple, yet a lot of people still fail to practice it regularly. It is easy to meditate anytime, anywhere.

You can enroll in a Zen center and receive guidance from a teacher, but you can also choose to practice Zen meditation on your own. You can meditate while sitting on a bus on your way to work or sitting in a coffee shop. You can simply pay attention to your breathing as you go through your day.

If you have a hectic schedule, don't worry because you can still practice Zen mindfulness. You may simplify the process by being mindful as you walk or take a shower. Being busy is not an excuse to avoid being mindful. If you are truly willing to do it, then you will surely find a way.

How to Practice Mindfulness on a Daily Basis

If you have never practiced mindfulness before, you might be wondering how to begin. Do not worry because this is a natural reaction of people who have never meditated in their lives. This chapter would help you get started as well as guide you towards finding your own mindfulness style.

Now, you must remember that there are numerous ways to meditate. However, your concern should not be to find the perfect form of meditation, but rather one that works best for you. This way, you would be able to practice mindfulness daily without feeling like it is a chore or burdensome task.

As a beginner, you can start with just a couple of minutes per day. Two minutes should not take up much of your schedule. After all, you probably spend a great deal of time procrastinating by watching TV shows, playing video games, scrolling your social media feed, or engaging in gossip.

Instead of wasting your precious time on these nonsensical activities, you should devote at least a couple of minutes to practicing mindfulness. If you think that you can devote more time to it, then you can start with five minutes.

The key is starting briefly. You should go from small to big if you want the new habit to stick. Once your mind and body get used to allotting two to five minutes for Zen mindfulness, then you can go ahead and add more time to your meditation session.

See to it that you choose a time as well as a trigger. It is up to you if you want the time to be specific or general. For example, you can choose to practice mindfulness meditation at 6 am every day before getting ready for work. Conversely, you can also choose to practice mindfulness meditation in the morning, regardless of what time it is. Go for whatever works best for you.

A lot of people find early morning and late evening best for mindfulness meditation. It is during these times when your mind is fresh and ready for being mindful. When you wake up in the morning, your mind is not yet bombarded with work or school issues. You have not yet faced anyone who may give you troublesome thoughts, such as your spouse, colleagues, or classmates.

Likewise, many people choose late evening for mindfulness meditation because they are finally able to relax their minds at this time. When you get home from work or school, you no longer have to deal with anyone who may cause you anxiety. You are already preparing to go to sleep. Thus, your mind is ready for relaxation.

Nevertheless, you may also choose to practice mindfulness meditation during other times, such as during your lunch break. If you have one or two hours of midday break, you can use this time to meditate. Close your office door, and do your best to relax. If you only have a cubicle, you can stay seated and close your eyes. Do your best to relax your mind and meditate, even for just a few minutes.

Once you have chosen a time, you should choose a trigger. It has to be something that you already do regularly. For example, it could be waking up in the morning and getting out of bed. The moment you get up and fix your bed, you should begin practicing mindfulness meditation immediately. You must do this activity before you do anything else, such as going to the bathroom to shower or going to the kitchen to eat breakfast.

Of course, you need peace and quiet to be able to meditate properly. Choose a quiet spot in your home. This can be a vacant room, for instance. It can also be your bedroom if you have nowhere else to go. Simply go to a corner or stay at the foot of your bed to meditate. See to it that you turn off anything that might cause unnecessary noise, such as your smartphone, alarm clock, TV, or radio.

Ideally, you should also talk to the people in your household if you do not live on your own. Inform them that you practice mindfulness meditation every morning, and you need to have some peace and quiet during this time. Ask them politely to avoid disturbing you when you meditate.

You may also go out to practice mindfulness meditation. Gardens, temples, parks, and beaches are great locations. If you like nature, you will find peace and solace in these areas. Just make sure that you also come prepared for possible external distractors, such as bad weather, animals and insects, or other people in the vicinity. You can bring sunscreen and an umbrella. Ensure that you are also dressed properly to keep you warm in cold weather and cool in hot weather.

Proper posture is very important as well. You can meditate while sitting or lying down, although sitting is more ideal since you might fall asleep if you lay down. Also, sitting is more practical in settings such as your office or outdoors.

You can try the half-lotus or full-lotus positions. They are highly recommended for meditation. Then again, you can still sit the way you want, depending on your comfort level. You can sit cross-legged or with your back against the wall. You can use a yoga mat or add some pillows or cushions if you are meditating on the floor. You can also sit on a stool, a bench, a couch, or your office chair, but make sure you are comfortable enough. Your comfort level is important so that you can refrain from fidgeting and being distracted.

When everything is ready, you may begin your mindfulness meditation session. Meditate for just two minutes. You can use an alarm clock or a timer to help you keep track of time.

Take note that this is crucial. A lot of people think that they can handle long hours of meditation when they are not. This is especially true for beginners. A lot of them tend to overestimate their capacity.

As a beginner, two minutes is already enough. Five minutes is plenty. Do not attempt to go beyond this because you may not be able to handle it. You might only exhaust yourself or lose focus. Fifteen to thirty minutes of meditation for beginners is not advisable.

Then again, once you get used to practicing mindfulness meditation, you can increase your time limit. Just make sure that you do it gradually. Allow your body to get used to the activity. Soon enough, you will be able to practice mindfulness meditation for thirty minutes to an hour.

The practice of mindfulness meditation is not a competition. There is no need for you to compete with other people or even yourself concerning how long you can meditate. You are not undergoing a test of how long you can stay seated on the floor with your eyes closed, and your mind focused on being mindful.

You are adjusting your time limit because you want to develop a long-lasting habit. In order to do this, you need to start small. You need to start with just a couple of minutes and then gradually increase your time limit.

For example, you can practice mindfulness meditation for just two minutes for one week. Then, you can increase your time limit to five minutes for the next week. You can increase it even further to seven minutes for another week. An interval of two minutes should allow your mind and body to adjust to the change.

You can then go for ten minutes for another week or two. Fourteen straight days of ten-minute mindfulness meditation can prepare your body for an even longer period of meditation. When you become successful in this, you can add five more minutes to your session. This becomes fifteen minutes of mindfulness meditation for three weeks.

If you think you can handle more time, you can move on to twenty minutes and stick to this time limit for four weeks or one month. It is up to you when you want to move on to thirty minutes to an hour. Again, there is no competition in meditation. You have to meditate based on your preference and comfort level. The key is having the self-discipline, determination, and willingness to stick to your new habit.

Keep in mind that it is necessary to focus on your breath. Always notice the way you breathe in and breathe out. When you inhale, observe the way the air goes into your nose and your throat. Then, follow its movement into your lungs and belly. Observe it as you exhale and let it out of your mouth.

As a beginner, you may have a bit of a hard time doing this. So, you may count with every breath to help you stay on track. Do not worry if you ever lose track. You can always start over.

You should also pay close attention to your thoughts. If you find yourself having unnecessary thoughts, gently bring your focus back to the present moment. It is common for beginners' minds to wander during meditation. Just do your best to stay focused. As you continue to practice mindfulness meditation, your mind would get used to it and no longer wander around.

How to Expand Your Practice

Once you have devoted an entire month to practicing mindfulness meditation, you may try expanding your practice. Here's how you can do this:

Sit and pay attention to your breath

Believe it or not, this simple act is already mindful practice. It is a way to train yourself to stay focused. You must sit in a quiet location for an adequate period of time. Do this on a regular basis until you get used to it.

Whenever you are stressed out, you must stop for a minute and pay attention to your breath. When the minute has passed, you can bring your mind back to the present moment.

You can also try to take a walk to clear your mind. Rather than worry about the things that you have to do for the day, you should pay attention to the sensations of your body and your breath. You should also observe your surroundings as you walk.

Each time you have a meal, you should focus on eating. Observe your food, its taste, appearance, and smell. Observe the way the food makes you feel. Focus on your feelings and sensations as you eat.

Tea is well-known worldwide to produce a calming effect. So, you can also drink tea as a mindfulness ritual. Keep your attention focused on your movements as you prepare and drink the tea. Observe the way the tea smells, tastes, and feels against your mouth. Stay focused on your breath throughout this ritual.

Furthermore, you can practice mindfulness as you do household chores. When you sweep the floors or wash dishes, you can stay focused and mindful. Pay attention to the activity alone. Refrain from thinking of or doing other things as you complete the task.

The Five Precepts of Buddhism

Those who are serious about adopting the Buddhist lifestyle tend to live with the five precepts. They have a shared objective, which is to achieve a state of enlightenment or nirvana. They do their best to become the best versions of themselves. They also believe that following these precepts will increase their likelihood of having a better life in their next rebirth.

So, what are these five precepts exactly? It is important to take note that these precepts are not rules, unlike the Ten Commandments of Christians, but rather lifelong undertakings that you must live by if you wish to become a better person.

1. **Do not kill**

   It applies to everything and everyone. So, you should not kill people, animals, and even insects. It is because of this particular precept that highly devout Buddhists stay vegan or vegetarian.

2. **Do not steal**

   It means that you should not take anything that does not belong to you. Some examples are money, food, and clothing. You should also refrain from hoarding items. In case other people need help, you should also be willing to extend a helping hand.

3. **Do not exploit or abuse**

You should not exploit or abuse anything or anyone physically, mentally, emotionally, and sexually. Highly devout Buddhists live a life that does not include sexual activities. Then again, you can still practice Buddhism even if you do not practice abstinence. Just make sure that your partner is also an adult who gives you consent. Moreover, you have to learn to be content with what you have.

4. Do not lie

Buddhists greatly value the truth. This is why you must never lie. Likewise, you must not keep secrets or hide vital information, especially if they would benefit the public. You have to stay clear and open.

5. Do not use drugs

It means that you should not use recreational drugs, psychoactive substances, and hallucinogens. Avoid anything that can change your state of mind for the worse, as this can inhibit your ability to be mindful. As you know, practicing mindfulness is a critical element of Buddhism.

Alan Watts and Zen Mindfulness

Most of those who practice Buddhism and mindfulness know Alan Wilson Watts, more popularly known as Alan Watts. If you have never heard of him before, he was a British speaker and writer who popularized Buddhism in the West. He moved to the United States in the 1980s to study Zen.

However, Watts had quite an unconventional point of view with regard to Zen, mindfulness, and Buddhism. According to him, Zen was a worldlier version of Buddhism. He claimed that Zen Buddhism was practiced by the Chinese because they did not like to sit around for hours and are interested in a philosophy that incorporates sex, work, and everyday life.

Watts believed in thinking for yourself and not following any pre-existing beliefs or established rules when practicing Buddhism. He also believed that Buddhism was an early form of psychotherapy.

Then again, instead of saying that depressed individuals tend to suffer from belief systems that are harmful and inaccurate, he said that humans, in general, suffer from belief systems that are harmful and inaccurate. In other words, everyone is somehow crazy. Hence, everyone can benefit from practicing Buddhism, not just those who are depressed.

Most people identify Zen Buddhism with an ascetic lifestyle that typically involves shaven heads and robes. They also believe that it includes vegetarianism and pacifism, with a major emphasis on sitting meditation or zazen. What's more, they think that they have to have a strict spiritual practice in order to achieve enlightenment.

Watts believed otherwise. He was a known adulterer, sensualist, alcoholic, epicurean, and smoker during his lifetime. He had a bohemian and joyful approach to the practice of Buddhism. He did not believe in following a specific lifestyle to reap its rewards.

With this being said, you can choose to follow Watts' approach if you do not feel comfortable following the conventions of Buddhism and Zen mindfulness. Zenism does not make any prescription on how you must behave. There is no need for you to chant, wear orange, be a vegetarian, or even believe in peace. You just have to see straight and directly, with a mind that is not blocked.

For Watts, Buddhism does not have a specific moral code. He did not encourage anyone to behave in a certain way. He simply advised people to cultivate a particular condition of the mind, and that is a liberated mind. After all, it is not likely that you would want to do any harm. So, if you are liberated from the requirement to be good, then you may be good. Then again, it should also be noted that living a life of "sin," such as one that involves drugs or crime, cannot help achieve liberation.

Watts also said that there is no need to practice meditation. He claimed that zazen was unnecessary. This is such a huge contrast to the typical notion of Buddhism. How else can you practice Zen Buddhism without meditation? Indeed, Watts' point of view became highly controversial and led to many attacks from the Buddhist community.

It was widely believed that the main objective of Buddhism was enlightenment or samsara. It involved floating above worldly concerns and not suffering from attachment anymore. It was about being detached.

However, Watts did not agree with this concept. For him, trying to be "above it all" and detached was being "drunk on Zen." Being detached does not mean being perfect. You can be detached and still experience problems, desires, and frustrations.

In order to free your mind, you have to detach from a particular set of ideas. More often than not, people become too attached to their family, friends, pets, job, and material possessions. They fail to realize that the more ordinary life is, the more Zen it is.

Watts taught his followers that Zen is merely an attitude or a life orientation. Likewise, he claimed that detachment does not involve inoculation from emotions. It is not necessary to waste emotions attempting to accomplish the impossible.

Conventional Buddhist philosophy involves the Four Noble Truths, which were discussed earlier in this book. Watts, however, had a different definition of such precepts. He was not interested in following any instructions for living. This was probably why he skimmed over the Eight Noble Truths or the Noble Eightfold Path, which were often viewed as invocations, suggestions, or instructions.

Instead, Watts concentrated on the spirit of marga, which was about the middle way or the balanced life. Incidentally, it did not mean "moderation in all things." The Middle Way should be distinguished carefully from mere moderation or compromise. In essence, it is the first life principle since everything, and everyone who is born comes from the union of two opposites. It refers to a balanced life.

If you do an in-depth study of Watts' concept of the Noble Eightfold Path, you would realize that it does not have a dictionary definition. The truth is that Watts' understanding of Buddhism was generally about being in tune with oneself and not having any desire to do wrong. It was as simple as this.

Key Points

- Zen Buddhism and mindfulness can either be practiced conventionally or unconventionally.

- It is up to you if you will follow the way of the Zen monks or the philosophy of Alan Watts.

- Buddhism involves precepts that help guide those who wish to practice it. However, these precepts are not like the Ten Commandments of the Holy Bible in the sense that they are not specific rules to be followed but rather lifelong undertakings that can help you become a much better person.

- As long as you can achieve your goal with Zen Buddhism and mindfulness, you are doing alright.

CONCLUSION

"When we get too caught up in the busyness of the world,

We lose connection with one another – and ourselves."

-Jack Kornfield

The quote showed above was from Jack Kornfield, an author and mindfulness teacher who co-founded the Insight Meditation Society with Tara Bach and Sharon Salzberg. He also played a significant role in introducing mindfulness as well as mindfulness meditation to the West.

What he said is true. Throughout this book, you have learned about Buddhism, Zen, and mindfulness. You have read about their history, evolution, and benefits. You have also learned how you can effectively practice mindfulness in order to reap its rewards.

It is through mindfulness that you can free yourself from your chaotic mind. It is through

Zen that you can finally be at peace. Whether you follow the traditional Buddhist teachings or not, Buddhism will still have a positive impact on the different aspects of your life if you take it seriously.

Allowing yourself to relax and let go is good for both your mind and body. You can be free from stress, anxiety, and even reduce your risk of physical ailments such as heart disease and high blood pressure.

When you practice mindfulness on a regular basis, your mind and body will get used to doing it. Eventually, you will form a habit, and you will notice your life becoming more peaceful than before.

On the other hand, if you allow yourself to get caught up in the hustle and bustle of everyday life, you will lose yourself. You will always be stressed and problematic, and your relationship with other people may get affected. This, in turn, can hurt your career, family life, and personal goals. Even worse, you can lose touch with yourself.

So, what should you do?

You need to practice Zen mindfulness. However, you should do it at your own pace and comfort level. This way, you will not be pressured to follow certain teachings or conduct yourself in a certain way.

At first, you may feel restless and uncomfortable. It is normal to assume that practicing meditation instantaneously results in inner peace. However, this may not be the case if it is your first time to meditate. Trying to be at peace may make you feel more chaotic than before.

You might constantly feel anxious about not doing it the right way, or you might worry about other people suddenly coming in and needing something from you. You might also be worried that your electronic devices would ring or give notifications; thus, disturbing your meditation session.

It is also natural to be anxious about missing out on something while you meditate. Someone might be texting an important message, for example. If you keep thinking about these things, then your mind will not concentrate on being mindful.

This is why you should not push yourself too hard. Do not force yourself to feel peaceful right away. Just let things be. Allow yourself to be at peace naturally, without pressure or force.

Once you get the hang of it, you will be able to improve. You will be able to sleep better and wake up more refreshed. If at first, your mind tends to wander during meditation or you usually feel sleepy afterward, things would get better on your second to the third week of practice. You will feel more alert and focused, even if you do not drink a cup of coffee beforehand.

Your mind and body will eventually get used to the peace and quiet that surround you. They will no longer give off the signal that it is time to fall asleep. Hence, your meditation session will not be interrupted. You will be able to complete every session without dozing off.

Then, when nighttime comes, you will be able to fall asleep faster, regardless of whether or not you meditated right before going to bed. You can meditate in the morning or afternoon and still get the same reward. As long as you meditated in the day, you will be able to have a relaxing sleep.

Other perks of meditation include feeling more confident and less rushed. Within a month of mindfulness meditation, you will notice that you are much less anxious yet much more productive. You will be able to do your work, but this time with more focus and grit. Since you no longer feel rushed or pressured, you can see the details more clearly and deliver more accurate results.

When you become more confident in yourself and your skills, you will get more things done. This, in turn, would give you an amazing feeling that would last for a long time.

Furthermore, your patience and mood levels will significantly improve. You will be much less moody than when you first started meditating. This would be evident in your daily life. You may no longer get cranky during traffic or while waiting in line. You may be more patient with colleagues, family members, and clients at work.

Through Zen mindfulness, you will achieve a sense of detachment. You will no longer have so many expectations; thus, preventing you from getting hurt easily. You will also be much kinder to yourself. The benefits of mindfulness meditation are truly satisfying.

So, if you want to attain peace of mind and be a better person in general, you should have an in-depth understanding of Zen, mindfulness, and Buddhism. This book is what you need to accomplish such personal goals.

See to it that you read each chapter carefully and internalize what you have learned. Share your newfound knowledge with other people so that they can also achieve genuine happiness and peace. Be an instrument to help people attain enlightenment.

I wish you the best of luck!

Thank you!

Before you go, I just wanted to say thank you for purchasing my book.

You could have picked from dozens of other books on the same topic but you took a chance and chose this one.

So, a HUGE thanks to you for getting this book and for reading all the way to the end.

Now I wanted to ask you for a small favor. ***Could you please consider posting a review on the platform? Reviews are one of the easiest ways to support the work of independent authors.***

This feedback will help me continue to write the type of books that will help you get the results you want. So if you enjoyed it, please let me know! (-:

Lastly, don't forget to grab a copy of your Free Bonus book "*7 Essential Mindfulness Habits.*"

Just go to:
https://theartofmastery.com/mindfulness

Resources

Living Zen: A Practical Guide to a Balanced Existence - Kindle edition by Segall PhD, Seth Zuihō. Religion & Spirituality Kindle eBooks @ Amazon.com. (2020, May 20). Amazon. https://www.amazon.com/Living-Zen-Practical-Balanced-Existence-ebook/dp/B0875KPX1K

Zen Mind, Beginner's Mind: Informal Talks on Zen Meditation and Practice - Kindle edition by Suzuki, Shunryu, Chadwick, David. Religion & Spirituality Kindle eBooks @ Amazon.com. (2010, November 9). Amazon. https://www.amazon.com/Zen-Mind-Beginners-Informal-Meditation-ebook/dp/B00I8USOM0

The origins of Zen Buddhism. (2019, August 31). International Zen Association. https://www.zen-azi.org/en/origins-zen-buddhism

Keown, D. (2019, February 28). *The Meaning of Nirvana in Buddhism Explained.*

Tricycle: The Buddhist Review. https://tricycle.org/magazine/nirvana-2/

Barbara O'Brien. (2018, December 24). *What Is Nirvana in Buddhism?* Learn Religions. https://www.learnreligions.com/nirvana-449567

Kane, L. (2020, May 9). *Buddha Weekly Special: Interviews with the Buddhist Teachers — Zasep Tulku Rinpoche.* Buddha Weekly: Buddhist Practices, Mindfulness, Meditation. https://buddhaweekly.com/the-noble-eightfold-path/

mindbodygreen. (2020a, June 29). *10 Tips to Find Zen In the Chaos Of Everyday Life.* https://www.mindbodygreen.com/0-21510/10-tips-to-find-zen-in-the-chaos-of-everyday-life.html

Cahn, L. (2019, March 27). *Chilling Reincarnation Stories: Meet 6 People Who Lived Before.* Reader's Digest. https://www.rd.com/article/chilling-reincarnation-stories/

BBC - Religions - Buddhism: The Four Noble Truths. (2009, November 17). BBC. https://www.bbc.co.uk/religion/religions/buddhism/beliefs/fournobletruths_1.shtml

Four Noble Truths | The Buddhist Centre. (2015, February 20). The Buddhist Centre. https://thebuddhistcentre.com/text/four-noble-truths

Staff, L. R. (2020, July 16). *Buddhist Teachings on Mindfulness Meditation.* Lion's Roar. https://www.lionsroar.com/buddhist-teachings-on-mindfulness-meditation/

Farias, M. (2015, June 5). *Mindfulness has lost its Buddhist roots, and it may not be doing you good.* The Conversation. https://theconversation.com/mindfulness-has-lost-its-buddhist-roots-and-it-may-not-be-doing-you-good-42526#:%7E:text=Mindfulness%20is%20a%20technique%20extracted,state%20of%20%E2%80%9Cbare%20awareness%E2%80%9D.

Mindworks Team. (2020, May 25). *What is Zen Meditation? Benefits & Techniques.*

Mindworks Meditation. https://mindworks.org/blog/what-is-zen-meditation-benefits-techniques/

Hutyra, H. (2020, June 21). *108 Buddha Quotes on Meditation, Spirituality, and Happiness.* KeepInspiring.Me. https://www.keepinspiring.me/buddha-quotes/

Crook, J. (2018, January 2). *Introducing Buddhism: A Guide for Western Beginners.* Western Chan Fellowship. https://www.westernchanfellowship.org/dharma/dharma-library/dharma-article/2000/introducing-buddhism-a-guide-for-western-beginners/

How to Turn Your Brain from Anger to Compassion. (2013, September 4). Greater Good. https://greatergood.berkeley.edu/article/item/how_to_turn_brain_anger_compassion

Pardon Our Interruption. (2013). American Psychological Association. https://www.apa.org/news/press/releases/2013/03/religion-spirituality

September 1, B. C. B. O. I. E. (2014, July 25). *Why People Turn to Religion and Spirituality? Positive Emotions as Leading to Religion and Spirituality.* Metanexus. https://www.metanexus.net/why-people-turn-religion-and-spirituality-positive-emotions-leading-religion-and-spirituality/

Todd, D. (2009, March 12). *Why people like Buddhism, and why some do not.* Vancouver Sun. https://vancouversun.com/news/staff-blogs/why-people-like-buddhism-and-why-some-do-not

Valentine, M. (2014, June 6). *7 Ways Zen Buddhism Can Change Your Life.* Buddhaimonia. https://buddhaimonia.com/blog/zen-buddhism

Why So Many Americans Are Turning to Buddhism. (2019, March 7). Pocket. https://getpocket.com/explore/item/why-so-many-americans-are-turning-to-buddhism

Purdue University Global. (2019, July 8). *The (Nontraditional) College Student's Guide to Mindfulness*. Purdue Global. https://www.purdueglobal.edu/blog/stu dent-life/college-students-guide-mindfulness/#:%7E:text=It%20improves %20overall%20mental%20health.&text= Another%20study%20from%20the%20J ournal,sleep%2C%20and%20better%20p hysical%20health.

Yoga, meditation improve brain function and energy levels, study shows. (2016, September 6). ScienceDaily. https://www.sciencedaily.com/releases/ 2017/09/170906103416.htm#:%7E:text= FULL%20STORY- ,Practicing%20brief%20sessions%20of% 20Hatha%20yoga%20and%20mindfulne ss%20meditation%20can,from%20the% 20University%20of%20Waterloo.&text= %22These%20include%20the%20release %20of,reduced%20focus%20on%20rumi native%20thoughts.

Pargament, K. (2013). *What Role Do Religion and Spirituality Play In Mental Health?* American Psychological Association.

https://www.apa.org/news/press/releas
es/2013/03/religion-spirituality

Selva, J. (2020, May 21). *76 Most Powerful
Mindfulness Quotes: Your Daily Dose of
Inspiration*. Positive Psychology.
https://positivepsychology.com/mindful
ness-quotes/

Buddhism at a Glance. (2009, November 17).
BBC.
https://www.bbc.co.uk/religion/religion
s/buddhism/ataglance/glance.shtml#:~:
text=There%20is%20no%20belief%20in,
of%20morality%2C%20meditation%20a
nd%20wisdom.

Babauta, L. *12 Essential Rules to Live More Like
a Zen Monk*. Zen Habits.
https://zenhabits.net/12-essential-rules-
to-live-more-like-a-zen-monk/

Valentine, M. (2015). *The Beginner's Guide to
Zen Living: 10 Steps to Transforming
Your Life with the Spirit of Zen*.
Buddhaimonia.
https://buddhaimonia.com/blog/zen-
living

Morin, A. *How to Know If Zen Meditation Is Right for You. Benefits, Uses, and Access to the Unconscious.* Very Well Mind. https://www.verywellmind.com/what-is-zen-meditation-4586721

Babauta, L. *How to Meditate Daily.* Zen Habits. https://zenhabits.net/meditate/

Lott, T. *Eastern Thought – A Beginner's Guide.* Tim Lott's Writing Blog. https://timlottwriter.wordpress.com/the-basics-of-zenism/

Brown, L. (2018, June 5). *How to Practice Buddhism: A No-Nonsense Guide to Buddhist Beliefs.* Hack Spirit. https://hackspirit.com/practice-buddhism/

Wikipedia. *Alan Watts.* https://en.wikipedia.org/wiki/Alan_Watts#:~:text=Alan%20Wilson%20Watts%20(6%20January,Hinduism%20for%20a%20Western%20audience.&text=In%20Psychotherapy%20East%20and%20West,as%20a%20form%20of%20psychotherapy.

Grothaus, M. (2016, June 2). *Here's How a Month of Zen Meditation Changed My Life*. Fast Company.
https://www.fastcompany.com/3060330/heres
-how-a-month-of-zen-meditation-changed-my-
life

www.ingramcontent.com/pod-product-compliance
Lightning Source LLC
Chambersburg PA
CBHW062133040426

42335CB00039B/2095